The Gridiron Game

❧

*An Anthology of
Football Writings*

❧

Edited by Dick Wimmer

A Division of Howard W. Sams & Company

Published by Masters Press
A Division of Howard W. Sams & Company
2647 Waterfront Pkwy E. Dr, Suite 100,
Indianapolis, IN 46214

© 1997, Dick Wimmer
All rights reserved. Published 1997

Printed in the United States of America.

No part of this publication may be reproduced, stored in a retrieval system, or transmitted, in any form or by any means, electronic, mechanical, photocopying, recording, or otherwise, without the prior permission of Masters Press.

Library of Congress Cataloging-in-Publication Data
The gridiron game : an anthology of football writings / edited by Dick Wimmer.
     p.   cm.
  ISBN 1-57028-153-X
  1. Football--United States. I. Wimmer, Dick.
  GV951.G75   1997   97-28447
  796.332'0973--dc21   CIP

Every reasonable effort has been made to obtain reprint permissions. The publisher will gladly receive information that will help rectify any inadvertent errors or omissions in subsequent editions.

Table of Contents

Acknowledgments
vi

Introduction
vii

George Plimpton
From Mad Ducks and Bears
1

Bill Cosby
From Introduction to I Am Third
5

William Goldman
From Wait Till Next Year
9

Frederick Exley
From A Fan's Notes
19

Jimmy Breslin
Y.A. Tittle's 176th Game
23

Allison Danzig
Dick Kazmaier
33

Contents

Red Smith
Joe Bellino
37

Dan Jenkins
From You Call It Sports, But I Say It's A Jungle Out There
41

Jimmy Cannon
From Nobody Asked Me, But...
53

Roy Blount, Jr.
From About Three Bricks Shy Of A Load
57

Thomas Boswell
From Game Day
61

Jim Murray
He Adds Perfect Touch
65

Steve Hubbard
From Great Running Backs
69

Dick Wimmer
Pro Football's Greatest All-Around Player
73

Pat Conroy
From The Prince of Tides
77

Ed Linn
Glenn Davis and Doc Blanchard
93

Contents

Ira Berkow
Riggins and Life Without Blockers
101

Jim Brown with Hal Lebovitz
Ernie Davis
109

Chris Cobbs
Winslow Hits Wall and Keeps Going
123

Chris Dufresne
Young Blood
125

Tom Junod
Montana Fading Out
143

Bill Plaschke
Doctor Provides a Shield for High School Athletes
159

Pat Jordan
Belittled Big Men
163

Tim Green
From The Dark Side of the Game
181

Rick Lipsey
How Zebras Get Their Stripes
191

Acknowledgments

Many thanks to Tom Bast, Holly Kondras, and Heather Lowhorn of Masters Press for their continuing support and joyful spirits.

Credits:
Proofread by Pat Brady
Cover design by Suzanne Lincoln
Cover photography by Christina Smith

Introduction

The leap in your throat as Barry Sanders goes juking left, right, left, shaking and baking so low to the ground, then stopping on a dime and exploding into daylight down the sideline. Or holding your breath as Steve Young lets a pass fly a split-second before he's buried under a blitz — and the long, high, tight spiral arrows 50 yards through the air to come floating down onto the cradling fingertips of Jerry Rice in full stride, a step ahead of the defender, as he glides into the end zone with that streamlined ease.

But for most fans, these vivid moments are viewed from far away, up in the stands, or removed, with replays, on the tube. Down on the field, the thunderclap of vicious, high-speed hitting is beyond belief: how these rhino-sized, finely-skilled, and superbly conditioned athletes can sustain the brutal pace of the game, keep blocking and tackling, and remain still standing, however bruised and bloodied, at the final gun.

Introduction

So are you ready for some football? A literary party? From the legendary pros to high school heroics, from the war in the trenches to the needles in the knees, from the best and worst places to play in the NFL to the role of the referees, I offer up this collection of splendid writing about the sport. It kicks off with a shimmering slide show, if you will, that features memorable stars in their pain and glory, then digs deeper to explore more common themes that reach far beyond the game through the prose of Pat Conroy, Roy Blount, Jr., William Goldman, Jimmy Breslin, Dan Jenkins, Ira Berkow, Jim Brown, and Tim Green, to name but a few.

Dick Wimmer

George Plimpton
From Mad Ducks and Bears

Alex Karras. "I guess the best part for me was the thrill I got seeing what great football players can do physically – to see what they *really* can do. It's breathtaking to see Jim Brown do things that the normal player can't. That's why the Pro Bowl game means so much to football players: we get to see the sort of company we keep. I guess the greatest thrill I can remember happened to me in a Pro Bowl game, and hell, it was a play where I didn't do what I was supposed to do. I was the goat, really, and yet I'm not sorry...

"In their game plan," Karras went on, " the other team decided that they'd run take-offs on me every once in a while – that is, influence me by pulling the guard opposite on a sucker play and hoping I'd pursue, which being an aggressive tackle I was likely to do, and then slipping the ball carrier, who was likely to be Jim Brown, into the hole I'd vacated. It's called the 'Oh shit' play, because that's what the tackle says when he realizes he's been suckered and pulled out of position and the fullback's ripping through his spot.

"Well, I'd been out late the night before – when it's Pro Bowl time in Los Angeles the players aren't much tempted to be in bed at eight – and I'd had a few drinks and I didn't feel good. Consequently, I wasn't as aggressive as I would have been normally; I didn't feel like pursuing that pulling guard. Well, the other team didn't know that, so they called the 'Oh, shit' play, with Jim Brown carrying the ball.

"Next to me in the defensive line, I should add, was Gino Marchetti. Greatest, roughest end there ever was. Brutal. He'd been out with me the night before. He had a headache, and he wasn't going to be influenced either. So the two of us stayed, and they ran Jimmy Brown right at us. His guards were gone. He had no interference. It's the worst thing that can happen in the sucker play, that the tackle is not influenced. Not only did I have a straight, unimpeded shot at Brown, but so did Marchetti. My greatest desire was to really put Brown down – the greatest running back ever – and I was going to kill him. So I uncorked as hard as I possibly could. Marchetti must have had the same thought in mind, because he went at Brown like he'd come out of a cannon. Both of us, and we hit him pow! You could tell he was hurt. He was knocked back about ten yards, his head snapped, and he was like a buffalo going down; he still had the ball but he was shaking his head. The defensive backs, they saw it too, and they began to swoop down on him, like scavengers, to pick at him...Marchetti and I, we were savoring what we'd done; we just stood there and gloated.

"Well, something happened. As Brown was going down, he caught himself. He shook his head a couple of times, and as the scavengers were barreling in on him, he regained consciousness and went eighty-six yards for a touchdown!

THE GRIDIRON GAME

The most fantastic, brilliant run I've ever seen in my life! I stood there, next to Marchetti, and we watched it like spectators. I suppose we should have finished him off when we had the chance. But I don't regret it. It was probably the greatest thrill I've ever had in football."

1962

Bill Cosby
ð
From Introduction to I Am Third

I have two special memories of Mr. Gale Sayers. Both will remain in my mind, I think, forever.

The first thing I saw was in, of all places, Hugh Hefner's house. If you can believe it, there was one day when I was looking for something to do in the Playboy mansion and a fantastic thought crossed my mind: have Hefner's secretary call the Chicago Bears office and ask them to send over some films on the Bears and Gale Sayers.

The Bears office responded quickly, and I had a beautiful time. While watching the movie I saw Dick Butkus eating up as many people as he could and I saw Gale Sayers get in and out of quite a few predicaments. But I'll never forget one play. Gale Sayers was sweeping to his right, moving around right end, and this hole opened up. I don't remember if it was made by a blocker or whatever, but it just opened up. And my feeling while watching was that Gale would never make the cut in time. Because, number one, he wasn't looking in that direction. And, number two, he was moving in another direction.

Bill Cosby

And the man made the cut.

And I just exploded. I mean, my arms fell off, my legs fell off, and my head rolled on the floor – that's how excited I got about it. Sometimes when you get excited about watching a beautiful thing happen before your eyes, your arms fall off...and your legs fall off...and your head falls off. And I turned around to the projectionist after I recovered myself and I said to the cat, "Back that up!" And he backed it up. And I said, "Now run it again." And he ran it again. And Gale did the same thing. And this time my legs fell off...my arms fell off...and my head fell off. And I sat there telling the projectionist, who must have thought I was crazy, to run it over and over. And I saw that thing, I swear to you, twelve times. And I still cannot believe that Gale made that cut.

Then there was the Pro Bowl game in January 1970, the National Football League All-Stars from the East vs. The NFL All-Stars from the West. And this time Gale Sayers was coming around his left end.

I was standing on the sidelines because I'm a celebrity and there are some groovy cats in Los Angeles who let me stand on the sidelines. I was standing there and Gale was coming around this left end. And there are about five or six defensive men ready, waiting for him, you know. And I saw Gale Sayers split. I mean, like a paramecium. He just split in two. He threw the right side of his body on one side of the field and the left side of his body kept going down the left side. And the defensive men didn't know who to catch. They just stood there. Then they looked to the referee for help, because there's got to be a penalty against splitting yourself. But there is not. Tony Quinn was with me and we both looked it up in the rule book and there's no rule against splitting yourself in half.

1970

THE GRIDIRON GAME

Note:

Despite playing just 68 games in seven years, Sayers was elected to the Hall of Fame on the first ballot. At thirty-four years of age, he was the youngest ever. He was voted to both the NFL's fiftieth and seventy-fifth anniversary all-time All-Pro teams, and most longtime pros call him the most exciting, elusive runner ever.

"My game was quickness. I had a great first two or three steps," Sayers said. "There was no excitement for me to go 65 yards for a touchdown or 90 or 103 yards on a kick return. Once you're in the open, anyone can run. That's not exciting. The excitement for me was the first 10 or 20 yards. What did you do to get in the open? Did you have to fake out one person? Did you have to stiff-arm somebody? Did you have to spin around somebody else? Did you have to run by somebody? That was the excitement."

Imagine if today's medical technology had been available then.

"I probably would have played another two, three, four years," Sayers said. "Every surgery I had, I was in a cast from hip to toe for ten weeks. Today, you don't even have a cast on. They do arthroscopic surgery and the next day you're in the swimming pool kicking."

Imagine if he had played on artificial turf.

"I played on mud and grass and dirt. I didn't play on Astroturf. I was quick, and turf makes you quicker."

Imagine if he'd played on a great team. Even with him, the Bears had just two winning seasons.

From Great Running Backs *by Steve Hubbard*

William Goldman
From Wait Till Next Year

Legends, when they are healthy, and when it matters, truly matters, always come through. Legends are *there*. And I was there, in Comiskey Park when the man who, for any Chicagoan, is the greatest legend played his greatest game. To put it as briefly as possible: I saw Nagurski.

He was the Bambino of Football.

Grantland Rice went on record as saying that he obviously was the greatest football player who ever lived because eleven Bronko Nagurskis could beat eleven anyone elses. The point being, the man had a certain versatility.

Opening game of '27, his sophomore year at Minnesota, he started at end. But tackle was the weak spot so he shifted there. He had surprising speed for his size — six-two, 230 — and also, for his size, shocking power. Red Grange used that word in describing what it was like to try and tackle the man. It was "strange; like getting an electric shock."

Why would you tackle a tackle? Because Nagurski played

both positions, tackle and fullback, and was All-American at both positions *the same year*. But that was not the full extent of his versatility. Many feel he was surely the greatest blocking back. Hard to prove. Some evidence exists. And if you were a sports fan of my time in Chicago, these numbers meant something:

1,004-101

Beattie Feathers was a Bear rookie in '34, up from Tennessee. And those were his numbers that year —1,004 yards gained in 101 attempts. Almost all of it on one basic play. You know the famous University of Southern California basic play, made famous by O.J.? Student Body Left and Student Body Right? That's what the Bears had. Except Nagurski was the entire student body. He would go crashing off tackle or around end, Feathers riding him, then exploding on his own.

Nagurski will never be remembered as a great passer, but he threw the most important pass in pro football history. It came at the end of the championship game of '32.

The score as the game was ending was 0-0. The Bears were in deep but the entire Portsmouth team knew that Nagurski would carry the ball so they bunched in and stopped him twice. The third time was the charm.

He got the ball, bolted straight ahead toward the masses, then, almost daintily, at least for him, retreated a few steps and passed to Grange for the winning touchdown. (Not a bad battery, that.) It brought the Bears their first championship in eleven years.

Hysteria followed. Wild arguments all coming down to a single issue: Where was the Bronk when he released the ball? Because in those days, you had to be five yards *behind* the line of scrimmage to pass legally. The Bears won the argument that day, but the echoes built well into the off-season, at which point two men, Halas and George Preston Marshall of the Redskins, decided to hell with it, let's let them pass from *anywhere* behind the line of scrimmage. That decision changed pro football forever.

It also made things a lot easier for Nagurski. From then on, one of the Bears' best plays was sending him up to the line, letting him jump, loft the ball to Billy Hewitt (who sometime lateraled after the catch). When he retired, one Bears book gives Nagurski's passing totals as 38 completions in 80 attempts. (Considering that Payton is 11 for 34 and is the best at that play today, 38 for 80 will do.)

But all this, the blocking, the passing, the line play, the shuddering runs — I have to interrupt myself to tell about just one. In '33, in a run for the championship, the Bears had a 10-7 lead late in the game when the Bronk, playing defense, was caught holding, giving the enemy a first down. Long pass. Touchdown. The Bears are down now, 14-10. Kickoff to the Bronk. He bucks up to the Bear 45. Huddle. And he's crying. "It's all my fault," he says. "Just gimme the ball." Muddy field. Shovel pass right. He grabs it, chugs down the sideline. Hit. Hit. Everyone bounces off. Picking up speed now. The goal line closer. Roaring. Touchdown. Bears win.

Only he's going so fast and the field is so treacherous he can't stop. At the south end of Wrigley was a dugout. In those days it was kept open. The Bronk slams into the dugout before coming in contact with a brick wall. Later, groundskeepers swore there was a dent in the wall. Surely apocryphal. But what is known is from that day on, and for as long as the Bears played at Wrigley, the dugout was boarded up during football season. A leading sportswriter described the run: "Those who were unlucky got in his way. Those who were lucky got out of it. The only thing that could stop him was a brick wall."

Which finally brought him down.

Now to repeat — all this, the blocking, the passing, the line play, the shuddering runs, all that unparalleled versatility is only of value, meaningful value, if it helps the team. The year before Nagurski joined them, the Bears won four, lost eight. His first year with them, they lost four, won nine. His last year with them they lost one of eleven. The first year after he was gone, they lost five. They won 70 percent of their games during the Nagurski years.

Pro football was like a heffalump when I was growing up, this weird thing that huffed along come Sunday. I remember in the playground, during the great Bear teams of the forties, arguing constantly their merits. What it came down to usually was this: Could the Bears, the 73-0 Bears, the four-time world champions between '40 and '46, *beat Notre Dame?* That was what I had to face. And the majority answer was this: They could not. Reason? Because the college teams *cared*. They played for love. And the pros were just a bunch of big fat guys who did it for money.

Hard times at Elm Place School.

I didn't really care. (I did, that's a lie, I knew how wonderful they were.) But I didn't care how great the derision because *I got to go.* As a consequence of my Uncle Victor's haranguing, my family got Bear season tickets from (I think) 1940 on. They were good seats. On the twenty. But not like my Uncle Victor's. His seats, having been present at the creation, were dead center. I can remember now sitting in his seat and following the fifty-yard line straight up to where it could cut me in half.

And we saw such players. Slingin' Sammy Baugh, most

THE GRIDIRON GAME

accurate of all passers. And Don Hutson, a legitimate legend at twenty-five.

And the Bears had Sid Luckman and wonderful runners — Gallarneau and Standlee — and whenever I raved on about them Uncle Victor would shake his head and say it: "You should have seen Nagurski."

God, I hated that taunt.

"You should have seen Nagurski."

Because I couldn't. He was gone. Retiring after the '37 season, becoming wrestling champion then of some pro world or other, finally leaving sports altogether, heading back to the Northland.

Every time I'd see a great run I'd ask, "Could he have done that, Nagurski?" Usually my uncle wouldn't even bother to dignify the question.

At nights after games I used to wonder: Was he real? Could they be true, the stories — not all the stories, no one really expected all the stories, but some of them, just some of them.

Please, just some of them.

In 1943, six years after retiring, first there were rumors, then the rumors were fact: War had sapped manpower. *Nagurski was returning!*

Ecstasy.

Then more facts: but not to run, never to run, only to help out at tackle.

Despair.

It was worse than not having him there at all. I watched him whenever he played. Big No. 3. At tackle. Big deal. I still don't know what a tackle's supposed to do. There's this snap and then everyone gets all squished together. I don't know what a center does, either. And guards I follow only when they pull.

William Goldman

Let him run, I thought. Just let me see him run.

But he didn't run. The season went on. The Bears were locked in it against the Packers. Season, as all seasons do, winds down. One game left. The Bears have to win it. Have to. If they do, they're in the championship game. If not, say hello to Green Bay.

But they will win it. It's a cinch. Because they're playing the worst team in the league, the winless Cardinals. Except in those days, these were still the Chicago Cardinals, the move to St. Louis still inconceivably in the future. And if you think of the Dodgers versus the Giants, that's what this was then. They always were playing for the blood-spilling rights to all Chicago.

The game was to be in their pen, Comiskey Park. We trooped in, my family, led by Uncle Victor. "Maybe Nagurski will play," he said on the drive in. "They might need Nagurski. Then you'll see something."

There was, as I remember, a certain distant logic to his pronouncements. Nagurski was listed all season as the fourth-string fullback on the talent charts. And then the game prior, the third-string guy got hurt. (This is all memory now.) So he was moved up. But it didn't really matter, once the game began.

November 28th, the South Side of Chicago, and the Cardinals were simply inspired. They owned the line of scrimmage. And their fans owned the air. First quarter, all Cardinals. Second quarter, still. Close, but they were better. And they knew it. And at halftime we talked about how we'd get it back together and kill them in the third.

But late in the third it was the Cardinals, 24-14. It was their day. The season was suddenly (we'd only lost once, up till then) dying on us.

Earlier, in the first half, the second-string fullback got

THE GRIDIRON GAME

hurt. And then, with the Bears trying to get something, anything going, they sent their fullback into the line.

Pileup.

Slow unpiling.

Everybody back on his feet.

Everybody except our first-string fullback.

And then (and I can see this as I write), far across the field, this lone figure got off the bench, reached for his helmet. And slowly trotted onto the grass.

Murmurs from the Cardinal fans. Murmurs that built. They checked their programs. It was No. 3. And beside me, my Uncle Victor, who was to die before his time, was out of all control, standing and screaming and pounding me on the back — "It's him — the Bronko — and they're putting him in the backfield — now you'll see something — *now you'll see something.*"

I don't know that I was ever so scared in my life. I was so frightened that after all the dreams, all my ridiculous fantasies, it wasn't going to be right.

And he looked, truth to tell, very slow as he came on the field.

And worst of all, I saw doubt in my uncle's eyes. " 'Course he's been away six years," he said. "A lot can happen in six years." Into the huddle now. Then out of it. Luckman, still for me the most brilliant quarterback, moves behind center. Behind him now, waiting, Nagurski. And in Comiskey Park, it was wild, because even though they rooted for the wrong team they were fans and they knew what everyone knew that Luckman was going to hand off to Nagurski for an inside run.

The Cardinals knew it, too — you could see them inching closer together. I sensed the disaster, I really did, and then I realized that Luckman was too much the master to ever try the obvious, that what he would do was either (a) fake to Nagurski and throw a touchdown pass over the bunched Cardinal defense or (b) hand off to Nagurski, who would do what he did that won the championship with the pass to Grange: fake the run and do the passing himself.

Luckman counts cadence.

The Cards are waiting.

The snap.

Luckman turns.

Hands off to Nagurski.

Who runs. But slowly.

Too slowly.

The Cardinals are waiting.

It's not a fake. It's nothing at all but a plunge at the line. Only the Cardinal line is there, surging forward, and as I stared I saw, after all these years, I saw Nagurski being lifted up into the air by the enemy. Frozen and helpless.

I just couldn't watch. I was so f---ing mad. At Luckman for being suddenly now — why now? — stupid. At Nagurski for coming back. At the Bears for asking him.

All my years of waiting, all my hope, and I get an old slug who is going to leave us with a second down and 12 to go, maybe second and 13. I had no way of knowing then I was entering into the high point of my life.

I turned back to the field. Second and 6.

And 6?

"What happened?" I asked.

"I don't know," the guy next to me said. "He sort of fell forward."

I didn't get it but I decided not to turn away again.

Next play. Same play. Or sort of the same play, it was just the Bronk taking the ball from Luckman and ploughing ahead and the Cardinals zapped him again — only not

THE GRIDIRON GAME

before he'd made a first down.

And suddenly I remembered what the great Grange had said about trying to tackle Nagurski.

"Strange."

That was the word he used. It was "something strange."

And now something strange was starting to happen down on the field. Because it was clear that the Bears had no tricks today. They were going with the old man. And something strange was happening in the stands, too. The sounds were imploring, all home fans sound imploring a lot of the time. But it was different. I don't know about this, but what I like to think is that none of us would have rather been anywhere else in the world that November afternoon.

He just kept attacking the Cardinal line and the Bears moved down the field. There is an image I thought that day and it's this: If you've never seen an axe and you've never seen a tree and the one is swung at the other, you have no way of knowing what's going to happen. Maybe the tree will give. Or maybe the axe will bounce away.

He didn't bounce away. And the Cardinals were behaving differently too, slapping each other on the asses, trying to fire each other up.

They were ahead but they were already behind. This force was coming at them from God knows where and they couldn't get out of its way. Now the Bears are near the Cardinal ten. And the huddle. And the snap. And Luckman turns. And he takes the ball, Nagurski takes the ball and slices through to the eight and then a half a dozen men hit him and he falls forward and crawls, crawls, and more and more guys are dropping on him, diving at him. And finally, they stop him.

On the one.

They huddle in their end zone and they're shaking their

fists and hitting each other but they know what's coming and they also know they are helpless, helpless to stop it.

We're all standing now, Bear fans and Cardinal fans and what I remember most is this: It was eerie. Everyone knew what was going to happen. We were all seers that Sunday.

The Bears break. The snap. Luckman turns. Hands off. The Bronk takes off. The Cardinals are the tree. He is the axe. They give it their best but the axe always wins.

Touchdown for the old guy.

That was the beginning of the beating. From being 10 down with the third quarter going, the Bears win by 11. Nagurski gains, in less than one quarter, 80 yards, maybe more. We're in the championship game, we win that too, he scores his final touchdown there, then back he goes to International Falls, this time forever.

1988

Frederick Exley
From A Fan's Notes

To those who understand the slightness of an American's traditions, the place of sports in his life, and New York City's need to make do with what it has (the stadium, for instance, is a nearly impossible place to watch football), the Yankee Stadium can be a heart-stopping, an awesomely imposing place, and never more so than on a temperate and brilliant afternoon in late November. The vivid reds and oranges, the plaids and tans, the golds and greens of autumn clothing flicker incessantly across the way where the stadium, rising as sheer as a cliff, is one quivering mass of color out of which there comes continually, like music from a monstrous kaleidoscope, the unending roar of the crowd. And where I have been in Los Angeles' vast Coliseum and Chicago's monumental Soldiers' Field and able to imagine it, I am yet unable to imagine a young man coming for the first time out of those dugouts at that moment just prior to kickoff when the stadium is all but bursting its great steel beams with people. I am incapable of imagining stepping out and craning my head upward at the roaring cliff of color, wondering whether it be all a dream which might at any moment come tumbling down, waking me to life's hard fact of famelessness. The stadium stays. The game proceeds. Autumnal mists set in. At half time the stadium's floodlights are turned on; so that the colors, with each change of light, change, too — become muted, become brighter again, like a leaf going from vivid green to lemon yellow to wine red to rust brown, reminding one that time is passing, that time indeed is running out. It was that kind of a day, that kind of an hour, when the Giants, losing 17-10 with two minutes remaining, came hurriedly to the line of scrimmage, eighty yards from a touchdown and a possible tie. (Frank) Gifford, whom I was of course watching, had neither thrown off his sluggishness nor played particularly well. Nevertheless, I knew that Quarterback George Shaw, who was substituting for an ailing Conerly, would make the play to him. I knew he would because men under pressure believe in miracles and see what they want to see. Shaw would not, of course, pass to the Gifford who was even now flanked wide to the left side of the field but to some memory of the ball player he once had been.

For a few delirious moments Gifford made me forget my fear and the crowd eat crow for their rumors of his lost heart. In the same way that Shaw perhaps threw to some memory of him, he became that memory. Running one of his favorite patterns, he caught his first pass by moving straight up the left side of the field, beautifully faking one defender to the outside. Abruptly cutting in front of another, he had, when he caught the ball, eluded both defenders and to the deafening roar of the crowd was at mid-field when he was finally tackled. Pummeling and pounding J. on the back, I shouted, "Atta way! Atta way, kid!" The next play was an all-or-nothing post pattern, i.e., the receiver runs full speed for the goal posts and the quarterback drops straight back into the pocket and heaves for those posts. Running swiftly and looking back for the ball, having lost the goal posts from his distracted vision and fearful of running into them, Bob Schnelker dropped a lovely, a high, thrilling, perfectly trajected pass. There was scarcely a moan. So sure was the crowd now that it was going to be their day, they seemed happily undaunted. Nor was I any longer upset. Now the Giants were at the line of scrimmage again, and again Gifford was flanked wide left. Running what seemed the precise pattern he had run before, and to another thundering roar of the crowd, he made the catch at about the Philadelphia thirty and was moving laterally across the field toward us, trying even as he ran to find a way by Philadelphia's two deep men, now converging on him, and into the end zone. The crowd was wild. The crowd was maniacal. The crowd was his. J. was the one who noticed Chuck Bednarik, Philadelphia's — there are no adjectives to properly describe him — linebacker. "Watch out for Bednarik," he said. Hearing J., I turned to see Bednarik coming from behind Gifford out of his linebacking zone, pounding the turf furiously, like some fierce animal gone berserk. I watched Bednarik all the way, thinking that at any second Gifford would turn back and see him, whispering, "Watch it, Frank. Watch it, Frank." Then, quite suddenly, I knew it was going to happen; and accepting, with the fatalistic horror of a man anchored by fear to a curb and watching a tractor trailer bear down on a blind man, I stood breathlessly and waited. Gifford never saw him, and Bednarik did his job well. Dropping his shoulder ever so slightly, so that it would meet Gifford in the region of the neck and chest, he ran into him without breaking his furious stride, *thwaaahhhp*, taking

Gifford's legs out from under him, sending the ball careening wildly into the air, and bringing him to the soft green turf with a sickening thud. In a way it was beautiful to behold. For what seemed an eternity both Gifford and the ball had seemed to float, weightless, above the field, as if they were performing for the crowd on the trampoline. About five minutes later, after unsuccessfully trying to revive him, they lifted him onto a stretcher, looking, from where we sat high up in the mezzanine, like a small, broken, blue-and-silver mannikin, and carried him out of the stadium.

1960

Jimmy Breslin
Y.A. Tittle's 176th Game

They both woke up before the hotel operator rang for them. Y.A. Tittle didn't move. He looked up at the ceiling. This was the last time he would wake up to play a game of football because he had made up his mind to retire. "Costello dogs," he said to himself. He could see the No. 50. A brown 50 on a white jersey. Vince Costello, the Cleveland Browns' linebacker, reddogs the passer a lot and it was the first thing Y.A. Tittle thought about when he woke up in an eighth-floor room of the Hotel Roosevelt Sunday morning.

It is like that after 27 years. You don't wake up and say, "I'm playing today"; you wake up and say, "Costello dogs."

Aaron Thomas, the end, was in the bed closest to the door. He got up and walked past Tittle and went to the window.

"Rain," Thomas said.

"Heavy?" Tittle asked.

"Enough," Thomas said. Thomas opened the window.

Jimmy Breslin

Tittle could hear the taxicabs down on Madison Avenue, their low pressure tires whining on the wet street. He reached over to the night table and picked up a thick blue-covered looseleaf notebook. The complete set of Giants' plays are on diagram sheets in the book and Tittle turned to a sheet that said "double dive 39" on the top. It is a straight ahead play and Tittle began to study it. You use straight ahead plays on a muddy field and Y.A. Tittle began to go over every one that the Giants use. The amateur whines and curses the weather that's going to bother his passing. Y.A. Tittle looked up football plays that should be used in the mud.

He studied his plays through brown horn-rimmed glasses that were perched on a big nose that caves in halfway down the left side. Patches of shaved gray hair ran down the sides of his bald head. In the back of the neck, the gray ran into deep criss-cross lines. He says he is 38; the deep wrinkles in the back of the neck tell you that 38 is just a number that he puts down when they ask him how old he is.

He had spent Saturday night the same as he has spent every night before a game since they put television sets into hotel rooms.

Right after dinner, Tittle came back to the hotel room, took off his clothes and sat down to watch television. He was dressed as he always is for television on the night before a game. In his shorts with the glasses on, a filter-tip cigarette in his hand and his socks on. The socks are always on.

"Lots of years," somebody said to him.

He shook his head. "Twenty-seven," he said. "That's just about my whole life."

"What do you do after tomorrow, give it up?"

THE GRIDIRON GAME

"I don't know," he said. "I haven't said anything about it. But this game tomorrow is important to me for a lot of reasons. A lot of reasons. I want to have a good day tomorrow so much...."

He wanted to have a good day because it was going to be his last. Y.A. had made up his mind that he was through. The last thing they like to do is stand and tell strangers who work for newspapers that they are finished with the business. But they tell each other, and Y.A. Tittle had told them in the dressing room that this was going to be his last game. That would do it, he told them, and on Saturday night Tittle sat in his hotel room and watched television and he kept thinking about the last shot he would ever get. No comebacks. No Cleveland next year. It was Cleveland now, and the career now, so go out right.

Now, it was 9:15 Sunday morning and Tittle put down the playbook and got up and got dressed for breakfast. He put on a white shirt and solid black tie and dark slacks. He reached into the closet and took out an olive green checked sports jacket.

"Still raining?" he said to Thomas.

Thomas looked out the window. "Raining pretty good," he said.

He took the elevator down to the lobby and walked into the Roosevelt Grill. It is a supper club, but the Giants use it for breakfast. Red-coated waiters served steak and scrambled eggs and the players ate quietly. When they were through, Allie Sherman, the coach, stepped up onto the bandstand. He smoked a cigar and he was in shirt sleeves. A green blackboard had been set up, with red stagelights playing on it.

"Now, once we get to pinch blocking, let each other know when they go back into a zone," Sherman began. He chalked

Jimmy Breslin

in plays on the board.

In the background, Andy Robustelli's voice could be heard. He was in the back of the room, with the defensive team.

"Remember," his voice said, "we got to kick his rear end in. Remember, kick his rear end in for him."

When Sherman finished, the players filed out. Then Tittle moved over to Sherman's table, put the playbook on it and sat down. Gary Wood, the young one, sat on a chair behind him.

"Well, what do you think?" Tittle asked.

"The Green Bay special should be the best," Sherman said.

"Uh huh."

Sherman put the cigar in his mouth and waited for another question.

"How do we block on the slant 34?"

"Two-on-one," Sherman said.

Tittle picked up a knife and ran it across the tablecloth. "Now the biggest frequency of dogging..."

"Costello," Sherman said.

"I know," Tittle said.

"This isn't a game you win with the big play," Sherman said. "We have to go straight ahead at them. The longer we have it the less he does." He was talking about Jimmy Brown; when they are as big as this one, they say "he" and never his name.

"Certain types of screens wouldn't be advisable today," Tittle said.

"What ones do you mean?" Sherman asked.

"Well, I don't think to the Frisco side is advisable."

"The Frisco side is all right here."

"I guess I keep thinking of Chicago," Tittle said. He meant

THE GRIDIRON GAME

1963 in the championship game. He tried to throw a sideline screen pass to Phil King, and Ed O'Bradovich, a Chicago lineman, intercepted it and ran for a touchdown.

Sherman smiled. "No, it's different here," he said.

Tittle nodded. "I guess I keep matching a play with a game," he said. "I got a game I can remember for every play that we got. That's the trouble when you've been around a little while. You remember too many games."

It was just like a business conference. There was no talk of "we've got to win" or no worry about getting hurt or how hard he belts when you let him get going for two or three steps. Just two guys sitting at a table and calmly going over technical things.

Football, when you do it for money, is like this. It is a trade, a job for money, and in all of New York few people ever have done their jobs better than Y.A. Tittle. They brought him into this town to pass a football and he did it well enough to bring the Giants to three championship games. But this year, with age taking a step away from him, and leaving him standing there a target for a lineman, he has done little.

John Baker of Pittsburgh got to him in the second game and tore two of his ribs loose, and after that the Giants were through and Y.A. Tittle had to gasp for breath every time he tried to pass. For the Browns, he was ready. The pain was gone, and there was a shot of cortisone in him to keep it out. The Browns were coming in for a game which meant the league title for them. Tittle was coming in after something, too. He wanted to go out of the town on top.

"You only know what it's like to play around here if you've played someplace else first," he was saying at the table. "This is the city for an athlete. I don't think I can remember a game I think is as important as this one to me."

Jimmy Breslin

The bus left for the ballpark at 11:15. Tittle sat in the back on the right, a thumbnail between his teeth, looking out the window. He ran a hand over the glass so he could see out. He looked down at the sidewalk. Rain splashed into a puddle alongside the doorman.

Tittle began to move his lips.

The opener, he was saying to himself. Open with a double dive 39. Wheelwright right at them. Straight ahead. And watch Costello. Watch what he does.

In the stadium, in the light green-carpeted dressing room, he put on a gray sweatshirt and sat on a stool and looked down at his legs. Tittle's legs are smooth-shaven, so tape can be put all over them and ripped off once a day. His toes stick together, with corns on the sides, the toenails black from 260-pound linemen stepping on them all year.

"I saw you in the first game you ever played here," somebody said to him. "It was on a Thursday night, against the Yankees." Tittle smiled. The guy was talking about the old football Yankees.

"What about the kids?" he was asked. "Do they think it's funny that this might be your last game?"

"I don't know," he said. "They're used to this business. Kids can adjust when they're used to things. My daughter now, she takes American history here. Then next week we get back to Palo Alto, she'll be having world history. Everything changes and she just keeps up with it."

Then he got up and started to get dressed, and the thumbnail came up to his teeth again and he began to think about another play.

At 12:45, a buzzer rang in the room. It meant that players had to get up and get ready to go on the field and everybody came around and tapped Y.A. on the shoulder and wished him luck and he sat there quietly and said thank you, and pulled on a cigarette he had cupped in his hand so photographers wouldn't catch him smoking. It was, it seemed, just another working day for him.

Then you shook hands with him and your hand closed on wetness. His whole palm was wet.

"What's this?" he was asked.

"This?" He smiled. "This is the business."

And a few minutes later, clapping his hands together, Tittle came trotting out of the dressing room, down the runway to the baseball dugout and then up the stairs and onto the field and there was a huge roar from the crowd when he came running through the goalposts and over to the bench. He waited while the Giants took the kick-off and when that was over, Y.A. came running on the field for the last big shot of his career. He wanted to go out of this city the way the good ones always do. The field was all right, and the rain was almost gone. He had a shot at it. A good shot at going out of this town on top. He bent his head into the huddle and called the first play of the game – a double dive 39.

Tittle took the snap, spun, handed the ball to Ernie Wheelwright and then kept going back, faking a pass. He kept looking over his shoulder at the Browns as he did. What he saw was no good. Their line jumped the Giants on this first play and Wheelwright ran into three or four white jerseys and right away you could see Y.A. Tittle was going to have trouble.

For the Browns kept getting that first step on the Giants' line and they stacked up runs and their halfbacks were all over the Giants' receivers. And on offense, they simply shoved everybody out and let him smash. He smashed and spun off them, Jimmy Brown did, and they were defenseless against him.

Jimmy Breslin

In the second quarter, with the Browns ahead, 3-0, Tittle went back and saw nobody open and then he said the hell with it. He took off on his own to the right and got to the Browns' 18. Ross Fichtner got to him near the sideline and tried to break him in half. Y.A. went down face first into the mud, but he pulled himself up right away. The referee was yelling about a personal foul and the ball was going to be put on the Cleveland 9. Now Tittle didn't hurt from the tackle.

On the second play, somebody was after him from the side, and Tittle ran straight up. Then he stopped and threw to Dick James, who was a yard behind the goal line. That put the Giants ahead, 7-3.

The Browns came back and scored. Ryan, their quarterback, was having a big day. Then Tittle was on the field again and he hit Joe Morrison on the Browns' 49 and now noise came down out of the three-decked green stands. Tittle clapped his hands and bent down in the huddle. He wanted Gifford this time, he told them. They broke out of the huddle and Tittle loped up to the line, looking over the Browns as he came.

Mickey Walker's gray pants were straining as he bent over the ball. The others were there, too. Bookie Bolin, Darrell Dess. At the snap, they would be coming back to make a pocket for Y.A. Tittle. Gifford was out on the right. Tittle put his hands down. The Cleveland halfbacks, Walter Beach, over on the left, and Bernie Parrish, on the right, were deep. They go even deeper when you show pass. Good. Tittle had called Gifford on a square-out to the sidelines.

Y.A. got the ball on the two-count and went straight back. Walker, Dess and Bolin came back with him and the white jerseys rushed at the three and grunted and slammed and tried to get through. Tittle turned around and held the ball up. Here was Gifford faking deep, throwing his head to the left, then cutting in one motion and running for the sideline, and Y.A. Tittle threw it at him and everything he wanted out of the afternoon was in the pass.

Gifford was at the Browns' 34 and he had his hands out and the ball was coming right to him when Parrish came running right by him and grabbed the ball and took off down the sidelines.

Tittle already was on his way over to the sidelines. You learn how to do this back in high school, in Marshall, Texas. You always get over there and cover the sidelines when you throw a pass out there. Y.A. Tittle put his head down and ran straight for the sidelines, at the Giants' 30, and Parrish was trying to get past that spot and into the open. Tittle came up and threw his body at Parrish's legs, and Parrish went up in the air and came down on his shoulder. The two of them skidded into the deep mud and then Parrish jumped up and clapped his hands.

Sometimes, it goes like that. Everything can be all right and you can know just what has to be done and how to do it, and you've done it a lot of times before and it has worked, and then when you do it this time the whole thing falls apart. It is like that in any business office in the city. Even the best in the place falls apart on something. Y.A. Tittle, who worked at his trade in New York as well as any ever worked, had just blown it all on a play called a square-out.

At the end, Tittle was on one knee in front of the Giants' bench, a blue hood thrown over his shoulders, his hands scraped and mud caked. The lights were reflecting off the puddles in the mud around him. Out on the field, Gary Wood was running the team and the Browns, scoring nearly every time they got the ball, ran up a 52-20 victory.

"How is it?" he was asked.

He shook his head.

"I'm sorry," somebody said to him.

"I'm sorry I couldn't give you something better," he said. "You people here have been awful nice to me."

He walked out of the stadium an hour later, in a black raincoat and black tyrolean hat with a red feather in it. He carried a brown-leather attaché case and he looked like a businessman coming home from work, which was what he would be from then on. This was the last shot of a career that went 27 years and he blew it on a play called a square-out. Y.A. Tittle said he was sorry he couldn't have given the people a little more. Professionals think that way.

1965

Allison Danzig
ಶ
Dick Kazmaier

Princeton, N.J., Oct. 27, 1951

Dick Kazmaier today took his place once and for all in Princeton's pantheon of football immortals with the Poes, Sam Whites, and heroes of more modern vintage.

In a personal triumph, rarely equaled on any gridiron, the 171-pound tailback from Maumee, Ohio, led the Tiger to a colossal 53-15 rout of Cornell before 49,000 thunderstruck and overjoyed eyewitnesses in Palmer Stadium.

It was the eighteenth successive victory that Princeton has gained since it last lost to Cornell in 1949, one triumph short of the best mark for the Orange and Black. It sends the Tiger out in front as the heavy favorite to retain the Ivy crown and onto its meetings with Harvard and Yale with excellent prospects of setting a record by winning the Big Three laurels a fifth year running.

The collapse of the feared Big Red team in the game of the day the country over between unbeaten powers was

Allison Danzig

brought about by a high-spirited, fierce-tackling and blocking Princeton eleven that manhandled the Ithacans and stormed in to overwhelm their renowned quarterback and passer, Rocco Calvo, who could complete only three of fourteen aerials.

But once again, as a year ago, when Cornell came here with a powerful team and was buried under a 27-0 score, it was Kazmaier who was the chief high executioner, with two touchdowns and three touchdown passes. This time the butchery was far more brutal, the most awful perpetrated upon the Red by the Tiger since Fritz Crisler's 1935 champions won by 54-0, and it was so because the magnificent Kaz reached the greatest heights of his three-year career.

So it was fitting that the great running and passing halfback should have had a hand and one of Charlie Caldwell's legs in tossing the Princeton coach into Lake Carnegie. Caldwell had said early in the week that the team could toss him into the drink if it gave him a victory today, and at 5:30, less than an hour after the end of the game, Capt. Dave Hickok, End Leonard Lyons from Mount Vernon, and Kazmaier grabbed him at the boathouse and gave him the heave-ho.

Coach of the year in 1950, Caldwell would appear to have a good chance of becoming the first ever to win the honor a second year running. Considering that Kazmaier is the only regular remaining from the offensive platoon of last year's champion eleven and six of the defensive unit were lost, the Tiger coach has worked something of a miracle in his job of reconstruction.

The man who has made that "miracle" possible is the player of whom Caldwell said in training camp before he had played his first game as a sophomore in 1949 that he was too frail for varsity football and dismissed him as just

THE GRIDIRON GAME

another member of the squad.

It was this same player, Richard William Kazmaier Jr., who gave one of the greatest passing exhibitions seen on any gridiron since the introduction of the pass in 1906. Eight times in a row he hit his receiver before his first pass was grounded, the last one he threw in the opening half. Six times more in succession in the second half he hit the bullseye, and he came out of the game with the astonishing mark of fifteen completions in seventeen aerials for 236 yards.

His three touchdown passes were for 45, 33, and 4 yards, the first two to wingback Dick Pivirotto and the other to Lyons.

Not only through the air but along the ground Kazmaier was tremendous. Against a team that had set its defenses to stop him above all others, he ran as he had not all season to gain a net of 124 yards in eighteen tries.

One of his runs was a 50-yard sprint on a reverse from the double wingback formation Princeton used so effectively, to set up his own final touchdown. His most amazing effort in carrying the ball was a 22-yard gain made on the way to the Tiger's first score. Trapped by three Cornellians as he started toward his right, Kazmaier reversed, evaded the tacklers and tore around the Red's right end to the 13-yard line as the Princeton stands cheered madly in appreciation of this indefatigable feat.

1951

Red Smith
Joe Bellino

PHILADELPHIA, NOVEMBER 26 — The first time they gave Joe Bellino the ball, Army's John Ellerson leaped upon his sternum and spread him like apple butter upon the painted meadow of Philadelphia Stadium. The second time, he faked a quick kick, spun to run to his left, and was hit from behind by a runaway beer truck named Bob McCarthy. On his third try he did no better, and up in the press box a man said, "Army'll beat this team."

Just then Bellino took the ball again. He shot through a gap near the middle of Army's line, veered to his left on a long slant through the secondary, and raced 58 yards before George Kirschenbauer hauled him down on the Army 42-yard line. Navy was off and rolling in the sixty-first engagement of its Seventy Years' War with the football paladins of West Point. That first daring dash by the swift and stumpy marauder from the Severn didn't lead directly to a score but in one stroke it changed the complexion of the struggle from Gray to Navy Blue. Taking the opening kick-

Red Smith

off, Navy was smashed flat by the same clamoring Cadets who had smeared the dangerous runners of Syracuse and Pitt earlier this season. Then a punt by Army's Paul Stanley pinned the Sailors down a yard from their own goal line.

There was Navy staring glumly down the throat of a howitzer, and then Bellino busted loose. Before the first quarter was over, Navy was in front, 6 to 0. At intermission the score was 17 to 0, and 98,616 witnesses had a premonition that this might degenerate into another rabbit hunt like Navy's 43-to-12 gambol last year.

Nobody could foresee the heroics the second half would produce, the wild excursions and alarums, the mounting tensions as Army came clawing back in a frantic struggle against the stubborn foe on the field and the coldly impartial clock hung up against a bright blue sky.

At half time it seemed a shabby show, in spite of the mildest, loveliest weather this production had enjoyed in years, in spite of all the elegant trappings of traditional pageantry, in spite of the exciting presence of the admirable Bellino.

Army had messed it up early through mental and mechanical error. After the Cadets smothered Navy's first action and forced a punt. Joe Blackgrove unwisely tried to field the bouncing kick with his back to an advancing horde. Smashed from behind, he fumbled away Army's first chance to attack. Stanley's fine punt repaired that damage, and after Bellino's long run took the ball into Army territory, the military braced and Navy tried a fourth-down field goal that Greg Mather missed. So it was still a scoreless game, but on the very next play Al Rushatz, the West Point fullback, fumbled the ball back to Navy. Needing 23 yards for a touchdown, Navy got 'em fast, Bellino slanting over for the last four wearing Kirschenbauer like a stole across his shoulders.

THE GRIDIRON GAME

There never was another one-piece-play like Bellino's big run, but in the second quarter he was a constant menace, butting the middle for short yardage — and slipping outside the tackles to wriggle like a brook trout through congested traffic. With Joe running and Hal Spooner passing handsomely, Navy pushed down into scoring range again and Mather made the score 9-0 with a 26-yard field goal.

As the first half sifted away, the Midshipmen put on still another foray, once more with Spooner passing and Bellino carrying. With 17 seconds remaining, the quarterback threw to Jim Luper, who fell across the goal line with Bill Sipos hanging on. Trapped trying to pass for two extra points, Bellino flipped the ball back to Spooner, who ran for the sixteenth and seventeenth points.

Navy seemed in complete control. The Army attack, such as it had been, offered little to cheer the 2,400 Cadets in the stands. West Point backs couldn't seem to get traction on the dyed green grass, kept falling before they reached the line of scrimmage.

Even the fire of the Army defense seemed damped after Navy's first touchdown.

Something happened between halves, though. The third quarter opened and it was a different game. With Tom Blanda's passes complementing the rushes of Rushatz, Glen Adams, and Kirschenbauer, Army drove for one touchdown and almost immediately set out after another. Again misfortune balked the Cadets; a penalty for having an ineligible receiver downfield on a pass play slowed one drive, and the score was still 17-6 when the last period began.

The jubilant Midshipmen on the stadium's west slope had just about had it. Now and then they whooped and brandished white caps aloft, but mostly they sat transfixed, watching and praying. Dick Eckert, Army's second quarterback, engineered a solid advance that Rushatz consummated with a dive into the end zone.

Now it was 17 to 12, with nine minutes remaining for Army to chew at a five-point lead.

Navy stopped a drive, then fumbled. Rushatz recovered for Army, 17 yards from victory. Yard by yard, cudgeling the line for short gains, Army ground ahead to the six-yard line. There a hasty lateral got loose, rolled back to the Navy 20. Blanda passed and missed, passed and missed again. The clock showed 1:55 remaining when his last throw fell incomplete and Navy took the ball.

The contest was over, needing only a final theatrical flourish. There was a guy on hand to furnish just that. Guy named Bellino. Unable to run out the clock, Navy punted to midfield. Blanda wound up for the last prayerful shot, took aim on Blackgrove and fired. Bellino got in front of the receiver, picked off the ball on the goal line and went swirling 45 yards back to safety as the curtain came down.

1961

Dan Jenkins

From You Call It Sports, But I Say It's A Jungle Out There

It was, of course, too Hollywood for belief. That UCLA's glamorous quarterback, Gary Beban, and USC's glamorous halfback, O.J. Simpson, could emerge in the same city, in the same conference, as the best players of 1967, was improbable enough. That they could also wind up battling for the national championship, the Rose Bowl bid, and the Heisman Trophy, all on one unbearable Saturday afternoon, was strictly from the studio lots.

The event belonged on an MGM sound stage with everybody singing *Buckle Down, John Heisman*.

But there it was that Saturday, the Trojans against the Bruins before 93,000 in the Los Angeles Memorial Coliseum and millions more on ABC-TV's national telecast – a game played for more trophies, titles, and prestige than any single college contest ever.

Of course, the game would have been immense, dramatic, historical, all of that, if it had matched total strangers under those same conditions. And it was equally true that almost every USC-UCLA game is worthwhile. But to bring two such dedicated enemies, two universities so close in proximity (10 miles) yet galaxies apart in image and attitude, down to so desperate an hour made the attraction all the more dazzling.

Consider first the ironies and contrasts of the campuses. Here sat UCLA, a sprawling state institution with an enrollment of 29,000 students of varying backgrounds, colors, politics, and ideals, and with generous portions of everything from hippies to Harlows, located right where, according to USC, it does not belong. UCLA is on a lovely rise called Westwood, just beneath the elegant neighborhood of Bel Air, a five-minute Mercedes ride from the dining, drinking, and shopping splendors of Beverly Hills.

And over there sat USC, older by far, the smug, conservative, private school, with all of its scrubbed, predominantly white, Protestant, slow-smiling, basically upper-middle-class types. Just look where it is, laughs UCLA – practically in the middle of Watts, for God's sake. Southern Cal's campus is in fact flanked by rows of condemned paint stores, auto parts companies, and junk shops, and only a few moments from the disenchantment of downtown L.A.

To the USC man, UCLA would never represent more than it was in its beginning, a preparatory facility for teachers, a school unhappily named Los Angeles State Normal in its infancy, a school that turned to basketball when it couldn't hack it at football, a school that deserves such card tricks as "FUCLA," the poor school, the school that gave us Tokyo Rose.

At the same time, UCLA finds it difficult to be troubled by anything those Wasps at USC think. UCLA is so vast that half of the campus could protest the world's wrongdoings and the other half wouldn't know it.

THE GRIDIRON GAME

Long before Gary Beban and O.J. Simpson, there were sports heroes on both campuses, particularly at USC. In the 1920s and 1930s, USC was turning out such immortals as Morley Drury, Erny Pinckert, Orv Mohler, Gus Shaver, Johnny Baker, Cotton Warburton, Harry "Blackjack" Smith, Grenny Lansdell, Ambrose Schindler, and Antelope Al Krueger. In the meantime, UCLA produced Kenny Washington and Jackie Robinson – yep, he was a football star first – and then Bob Waterfield in the 1940s. But it wasn't until Red Sanders turned the Bruins into a national power in the 1950s that the Trojans had to take UCLA seriously, every season.

As for the coaches in this year's Game of the Century, USC's John McKay and UCLA's Tommy Prothro, they were as different as the campuses they represented.

Prothro was bigger, taller, older, and had been a head coach five years long than McKay. He was more secretive. McKay was generally open and friendly, a wisecrack artist in his profession. It was easy to imagine Prothro as a rancher. It was just as easy to imagine McKay, a careful dresser who leaned toward sun-bleached slacks, as a golf pro. Among their colleagues, Prothro most closely resembled Alabama's Bear Bryant in drawl, manner, and attitude. Quick, talkative, and well organized in the contemporary, gray-flannel way, McKay was similar to Texas's Darrel Royal.

There was an equally distinct difference between the two players who had brought their teams to high national ranking – the halfback, Simpson, who rolled right over you, and the quarterback, Beban who rolled around you.

For the seven and a half games of the season that Orenthal James Simpson had been whole, he had seemed to possess the finest combination of speed and power within the memory of any pro scout. He rushed for 1,238 yards in that span, and until his mishap in the Oregon game – a sprained instep that knocked him off his feet and onto crutches – he was a good bet to break the NCAA yardage record (which he would, indeed, break a year later). Not only did he crash repeatedly into stacked defenses and still wedge his way out and slice and dart for yardage, he caught passes and threw them at the least expected moments.

Coaches, scouts, and writers tried to figure out all season who it was Simpson's running style reminded them of. He exhibited the raw burst of speed that Mel Renfro had in college and some of the deceptive moves of Gale Sayers. But he also slammed in there and broke tackles like Jim Brown. Given daylight, he slid through with the nifty balance of Jon Arnett.

Gary Beban, the UCLA answer to Orange Juice, was one of those athletes who did things with infuriating ease. He passed with classic form, and he ran gracefully, almost in slow motion except that he managed to turn the corners and slide through. When his passes were in the air, the ball somehow looked longer, and the spiral was perfect, as if Beban had figured out exactly how many rotations it should make. His ball handling was superb, his faking even better, But above everything else, Beban had poise.

Prothro often said that Beban could beat you with a run, pass, fake, or call, and that his ability to change plays at the scrimmage line was perhaps his finest asset. A familiar sight for three seasons was Beban behind the center, shifting his backs, then checking, raising his head to survey the defense and shouting another play that unfolded perfectly. In the clutch.

Since early in the season when USC and UCLA attained their top-level rankings in the national polls, trying to rate their strengths and deficiencies had been a parlor game.

THE GRIDIRON GAME

You gave USC a point for offense, UCLA got quickness. USC had a better blocking line, but UCLA had a better pursuing defense. UCLA had the best passing, but USC had the best receiving. The kicking was even, the coaching was even, and there was no home-field advantage.

So who would win? A day before the game, a man who should be able to judge the situation well, John McKay himself, went to a blackboard and evaluated the two teams, player by player. He had a point grading system for this, and when he was through adding point by point, he totaled the figures for each team. Just like in the Hollywood script, they came out exactly equal. When that happened, McKay stepped back from the blackboard and made the least newsworthy comment of the most exciting football season Los Angeles had ever known:

"It's going to be a helluva game," he said.

In the end, the difference was that this guy with a name like a Russian poet, Zenon Andrusyshyn, couldn't place-kick the ball over this other guy with a name like the president of the Van Nuys Jaycees – Bill Hayhoe. Andrusyshyn would try to side-boot a field goal or extra point for UCLA, and Hayhoe, who happened to be 6'8", would rise up. The ball would go splat, plink, or karang. The last time Hayhoe did it, he tipped the leather just enough to make the Bruins fail on a precious conversion, and USC got away with a 21-20 victory in a spectacle that will be remembered for ages, or at least as long as German-born, Ukrainian, Canadian-bred soccer-style kickers play the game.

Of course, it was not exactly fair to insinuate that Zenon Andrusyshyn, the German-Ukrainian-Canadian, was the goat of the whole desperate afternoon. Though only a sophomore, he was a splendid kicker who boomed punts into the California heavens all day, and it appeared that if the ball were given time to rise, he was capable of place kicking one more than 60 yards. Rather, it was more accurate to give credit to USC's John McKay for one of those little coaching touches that sometimes supplies a subtle edge. This time it proved to be a subtle edge that gave McKay the most important game of his life.

"We knew he kicked it low, so we just put the tallest guy we had in there on defense," said McKay later, in what may have been the happiest dressing room since showers were invented. "We told the kids it wasn't so important that they bust through and make him rush the kicks as it was just getting to the scrimmage line and raising their arms high."

In his wry, twinkling, way, McKay then lit a cigar and said, "I call that brilliant coaching."

Although neither O.J. nor Beban was 100 percent perfect physically, both were superb in clutch after clutch. While he practically had to crawl to the sideline no less than five times to regain his breath because of his injured ribs, Beban whirled the Bruins to three touchdowns, passing for more than 300 yards, giving his team a 7-0 lead in the first quarter, a 14-14 tie in the third, and a 20-14 lead in the fourth.

Meanwhile, Simpson, his right foot throbbing inside a shoe with a special sponge cover, wearily hobbled away from piles of brutal tacklers and eventually managed to race for a total of 177 yards, including the touchdowns that put the Trojans ahead 14-7 and finally 21-20.

Had the Heisman Trophy award, therefore, really been decided by a couple of young men named Zenon Andrusyshyn and Bill Hayhoe? As Jim Murray of the *Los Angeles Times* said, "They should send the Heisman out here with two straws."

For almost the first 20 minutes it looked as if UCLA was the only team in the coliseum. The Bruins were a lot quicker

THE GRIDIRON GAME

in the line, niftier in execution, more confident in their game plan, and more inventive in their attack. Beban had thrown the first of 16 completions to his left end, Dave Nuttall, who would catch seven, and he had gotten 11 big yards on a keeper, and he had lead the interference for Greg Jones's blasting 12-yard touchdown run, which put UCLA out front. At the same time, the Trojans had not been able to move. In five possessions they had not scratched out a first down. On his first 10 carries, even behind an occasional and surprising eight-man line that McKay thought would unsettle Prothro, O.J. Simpson had gained only 11 measly yards. He had come no closer to breaking clear than Andy Williams, who was there to sing at halftime.

The situation looked normal; Prothro had McKay's number, just as everyone had been saying at the Daisy, the Factory, La Scala, and Stefanino's before diverting conversation back to who got which part in what TV series. It was normal except for one thing: USC did not have any yards or first downs, but it had seven points.

On the last play of the first quarter, just as it looked like Beban was cranking up the Bruins again, the UCLA quarterback threw a pass at midfield into the wide left flat. The receiver was open, as Bruin receivers were all day, but the ball hung. It may have hung because Beban's side, injured in the Washington game the previous week, prevented him from slinging the ball hard when he had to. It may have hung because he misjudged the risk of an interception. Whatever the reason, USC's Pat Cashman saw it coming. He darted in front of Greg Jones, leaped, and took the ball with nothing but 55 yards of beautiful, unpopulated coliseum turf before him.

While Pat Cashman's interception perked up the USC rooters – hundreds of whom, like UCLA's had been in the stands since dawn to get good seats – it did not seem at the time to be all that important; it might hold down the score, maybe. Sure enough, after a wiggly, 42-yard punt return by UCLA's Mark Gustafson, the Bruins were quickly threatening again, with a first down on the 15. But now a series of strange things happened that changed the game for the rest of the day. In three plays the Bruins got nowhere, and on the third one Beban got the first of the deadly blows in the ribs – this one courtesy of Pat Cashman – that would send him writhing toward the sideline. Andrusyshyn came in and missed a field goal from the 20. The kick was not one of those molested by Bill Hayhoe; Zenon simply side-winded it off to the left. And on USC's first play from its own 20, the game suddenly had another offensive team. Earl "the Pearl" McCullouch started it by streaking down the sideline off a daring reverse for 52 yards. McCullouch then caught a 13-yard pass. And now Simpson was warmed up. From 13 yards out, O.J. burst over guard for the touchdown – one that was especially vital, for it proved to the USC offense that it could move the ball.

Still, if UCLA was impressed it did not act it. The Bruins took the kickoff amid the most noise since D-day, and Beban promptly threw a 48-yard pass to Nuttall. It was first down on the Trojan 15 again. But, just like the time before, USC's defense got riled. Beban was smacked by everybody but Southern California President Norman Topping, one of nine losses he would suffer, and he had to retreat to the bench again. In came Andrusyshyn for the first of two field-goal tries that Bill Hayhoe would block.

As had been said so many times about Beban, he learned from mistakes. He could hardly wait for the second half to start to take advantage of Pat Cashman, who had intercepted him and who had buried his red USC headgear into Beban's lung. With only two minutes gone in the third quarter, Beban laid a perfect 47-yard pass into the hands of halfback George Farmer for the tying touchdown.

"Cashman had been waiting for another of those flat passes, so we sent Farmer straight down, right past him," said Gary afterward. "It balanced out. Cashman's interception was really responsible for our second touchdown." Between this score and the one that put UCLA ahead early in the fourth quarter, Prothro's team blew another excellent opportunity. The combination of a poor punt by USC's Rikki Aldridge, who redeemed himself for his and all other misdeeds of a lifetime by ultimately kicking the game-winning conversion, and a Beban pass put UCLA on the Trojan 17. It was there that Hayhoe, a junior from Van Nuys who weighed 254 along with his 6'8", lumbered through to drop Beban for a whopping loss, and two plays later he blocked another field-goal attempt by the Ukrainian.

"Those things somehow weren't as discouraging then as they are now," said Beban later as he wandered around in the USC locker room, sipping a canned Coke, smiling, and congratulating the Trojans. "We knew we would score again."

They did. Beban hit four passes in a brisk seven-play drive covering 65 yards, the last one going to Nuttall for 20 yards and the touchdown that made it 20-14 with only 11 minutes remaining. Andrusyshyn missed the point because Hayhoe had gotten a finger on it, and while it occurred to everybody in the Western world that this could be a pretty unfortunate point to miss, UCLA still looked like the better team. The Trojans had not seriously threatened. Junior Steve Sogge had given way to senior Toby Page at quarterback, and it was no Los Angeles secret that John McKay's wife, Corky, was a better passer than Page. Nor had O.J.

really busted loose.

But now it was time for Simpson to get back in the Heisman derby, thanks to a thing called 23-Blast. UCLA's tough tacklers had been kindly helping O.J. back up on his feet all day, a fine sporting gesture with the subtle design of keeping Simpson from resting. And at last it was time for O.J. to knock them down. And out.

It was third down at his own 36 when Toby Page saw UCLA's linebacker move out, anticipating the play Page had called in the huddle. Page checked signals and called another play at the line. It was 23-Blast. As it unfolded, it looked like a five-yard gain. Guard Steve Lehmer and tackle Mike Taylor cleared O.J. through the hole. Then Simpson veered out toward the left sideline. Oh, well, a 15-yard gain and a first down. But end Ron Drake screened off UCLA's halfback, and the safety sucked over, and, hey, what's this? O.J. angled back to the middle, to his right, and a great glob of daylight became visible. And then he was running like the 9.4 sprinter he is, despite that sore foot and that funny shoe, and there was not anybody down there for the rest of the 64 yards who was about to catch him.

Of the remarkable 1,415 yards Simpson gained that season, those 64 were the most impressive of all, for they came after two hours of the toughest punishment he had endured – and they stretched all the way to No. 1.

About an hour and a half after the game, down in the USC dressing room, which had finally emptied and grown as quiet as it had been before the kickoff, a brief scene was enacted that served as a fitting epilogue. Dressed now, blazers on, hair combed, refreshed, Gary Beban and O.J. Simpson met, looking like two young men anticipating a fraternity council meeting.

"Gary, you're the greatest," said O.J. "It's too bad one of

THE GRIDIRON GAME

us had to lose."

"O.J., you're the best," said Beban. "Go get 'em in the Rose Bowl."

O.J. grinned. Presently, he ambled down the hall, through a door, and up a walkway to an exit gate where clusters of USC fans were still gathered. It was roughly, oh about 64 yards.

1967

Jimmy Cannon
From Nobody Asked Me, But...

The football field becomes Johnny Unitas' quiet lawn when he walks on it. It is as though he moved across his own grass with that bowlegged saunter. The screams of the buffs don't seem to reach him. The excitement subsides around him as he strolls toward the center's rump. The great quarterback acts as if he is in some private place.

What Unitas accomplishes is often thrilling. But there are instances when all that is happening in a big football game appears to bore him. It is as though he can establish a personal solitude in a congested stadium. The people coming at him don't exist. All that concerns him is handing or flipping the football to a guy who runs with it or throwing it to a receiver to catch.

Time doesn't harass him. The clock may be full of minutes, or short of seconds. Unitas doesn't hurry. He does it fast, but desperation doesn't goad him. The loose-boned gait suggests that he is stalling even when he is causing

Jimmy Cannon

the excitement to happen. There will be times when the Rams will get to Unitas when they play the Colts for the championship of the Coastal Division in Los Angeles. It will not disturb his poise.

On the next play he will stand there as if he was far beyond their rush, and he will do his work with a casual elegance. His serenity suggests contempt for the people trying to get their hands on him to throw him around. He also knows that he must stay in the pocket formed by his blockers. The great quarterback doesn't run well with a football under his arm.

The Colts are unbeaten because Unitas is what he used to be. The right elbow hurts him. It restricts his practice, and the action of throwing cuts him with a knife of pain every time he passes. The limited time for rehearsal should cripple his timing but it hasn't. Some of his regular receivers have been laid up. But he throws just as well to such as Willie Richardson, Alex Hawkins and Ray Perkins.

The runners find dents in the line. They get around the ends. It has to be because Unitas is throwing as well as he did when the Colts beat the Giants in 1958 and 1959 for the championship of professional football. The runners go further because the other people must scatter to try to stop the pass.

"I can't relax when Unitas is out there," said Vince Lombardi who coaches the Green Bay Packers. "I'm scared to death while he's on the field."

He has reason to be. It was Unitas who beat the Packers, 13-10, in Baltimore on November 5. There was 1:26 left and Baltimore was on Green Bay's 23-yard line. In the huddle, Willie Richardson told Unitas he could beat Herb Adderley. The ball was thrown to Richardson on the 2-yard line, and the end went into the end zone standing up as

THE GRIDIRON GAME

Adderley dove for him and missed.

"John threw it low and away," explained Richardson. "There was no way Adderley could get to it. He had to dive."

Rage doesn't change Unitas, or elation. He ducks into the shower room to shave after a good game or a bad one. He seems to be getting himself together to be sure he will not permit emotion to maim his replies in the prolonged interview that follows every game on the Colts' schedule. The answers are careful and precise, and he can read them the next day without regret.

It is a remembrance of techniques. It is more like a plumber telling his old lady about a job than the highest paid football player in sports describing his part in a celebrated event. The talk is often traced with wit which comes in the disguise of cliché.

In 1965 the surgeons cut into Unitas' knee. His shoulder was hurt in 1966, but he played. The Colts were contenders until the Packers caught up with them in Baltimore. The Colts were inside the 10 with nine minutes to play and proceeding toward what could have been the deciding touchdown. But Unitas couldn't locate a receiver, and had to use his legs.

It was Willie Davis who hit him, and jostled the ball out of his embrace. It was picked up by Dave Robinson, and that was as far as the Colts got last year.

Always it is Davis who brings trouble to Unitas. This Sunday Deacon Jones and Lamar Lundy, the Los Angeles ends, could ruin him. The Rams don't have to blitz much with Jones and Lundy coming at him from both sides. The tackles, Roger Brown and Merle Olson, figure to pile up Unitas, too.

But this I know. Johnny Unitas will get up and do what he has to do on the next play, and no one does better when

Jimmy Cannon

it is breaking right for him. And when it's over he won't attempt to make it dramatic or funny. He'll put on his street clothes and pack his public character in the canvas bag with his football gear. There is no actor in him, or comedian or poet. He is all quarterback.

Johnny Unitas seems to vanish when he goes out through the players' gate. He is only conspicuous during a football game.

1967

Roy Blount, Jr.
From About Three Bricks Shy Of A Load

I enjoy watching Lynn Swann dance with the ball.

Whenever I see Swann hang and twist inimitably in the air to snatch a pass away from glowering, jealous defenders, I think of W. C. Fields stomping away from a Charlie Chaplin movie, growling, "The son of a bitch is a ballet dancer."

Swann began to take dancing lessons when he was in the fourth grade, at his mother's insistence. His mother had always wanted a girl, so she made him dance, after naming him Lynn. What a name to play football under! Lynn Swann. First name girlish, last name not only birdlike but Proustian; and all those extra n's trailing around. Why do wide receivers get stuck with names like Lynn Swann and Golden Richards?

"The first day of school, every year, there I was listening to them call the boy's names," says Swann. "And every time, they'd call all the boys, and I'd think, 'Oh, God, I'm on the girls' list again.'"

Fortunately, Lynn's older brother Calvin "was a year ahead of me, but then he had mononucleosis real bad, and one day he was showing off in front of his class and swallowed a straight pin, which they never did find, so altogether he was sick in the hospital ten months. So from then on we were in the same class. And when people got on me about my name or dancing, Calvin beat up a couple of people, and everything was cool."

However, in 1975 when he was a rookie, Swann decried the notion, advanced by an older Steeler, that Mean Joe Greene was a "big brother" who whipped on opponents so that other Steelers could do their thing. It was true that in those days the Steelers overpowered the rest of the league primarily by defensive intimidation, and Greene was the head intimidator.

Greene on the field was in some ways Fieldsian: irascible, unaccountably deft for his bulk, and generally overbearing. The Steeler defense, still featuring Greene but now better typified by the fuming, slashing middle linebacker Jack Lambert, remains crucial, but the team's most spectacular element this year has been its passing attack, of which Swann is both the steadiest and the niftiest element.

And Swann on the field is Chaplinesque: small, frequently pummeled, bouncing, poignant but uncrushable, a tough little nut sometimes lighter than air.

Swann is also one of the few people in the NFL who can be identified in any significant way with freedom of expression. In 1976 he had the temerity to complain about the fact that, even when he was nowhere near the ball, defensive backs were belting him viciously in the head and giving him concussions. "The game is tough enough within the rules," he said, and if the cheap shots continued he would quit the game.

THE GRIDIRON GAME

The subsequent uproar involved fines, lawsuits, rules changes and wide spread denunciations of Swann (even sometimes, privately, by his teamates) not only as a prima donna California big shot who appeared on television too often but also as a sissy, a punk, a tattletale and a crybaby. Fortunately a boy named Lynn gets inured to that kind of talk.

Furthermore, his receiving style is so distinctive that he doesn't have to do post-touchdown gyrations. He makes over three-fourths of his catches over the middle, where small, fleet receivers have traditionally been less than avid to tread. And he excels at such unobtrusive aspects of his position as running correct patterns and blocking.

On the other hand, at the University of Southern California he majored in public relations. He wants to be on camera, isolated, doing amazing things with the ball. When his somewhat less acrobatic but equally effective receiving mate John Stallworth catches a touchdown pass and Swann appears on the screen empty-handed, Swann does not always appear to be a hundred percent pleased. When Stallworth was catching ten passes against Denver in the playoffs, Swann's thought, he says, was "That's supposed to be me doing that."

He also wishes that pass receivers weren't so dependent on the passer.

"Before this year," he observes, "people were saying, 'Lynn Swann is making such great catches, he's making Bradshaw look good.' All of a sudden Terry has a great year, and people go back to the typical attitude, that the quarterback is the guy who completes the pass.

"That's why receivers tend to be such loners. In high school in San Mateo, Jesse Freitas and I were a big passing combination. My senior year he went to Stanford. When I graduated, people wanted me to go there so we could team up again, but I went to USC because he wasn't there. You don't want to go on not knowing whether it's you being that good or the quarterback."

Perhaps most receivers are too sensitive about being regarded as "little guys hanging out there on the end," as Swann puts it, to risk complaining about being illegally mauled. After Swann had spoken out, the retired great receiver Lance Alworth declared that he always considered cheap shots to the head a compliment to his ability.

"I don't want a compliment," says Swann sensibly, "that could end my career." His protests led to rules limiting defenders' jostling of receivers and to the league's practice of scrutinizing game films and fining people whom the films revealed to be behaving too savagely.

"I think if you do a study of well-known cheap-shot artists," Swann says, "you'll find that a number of them this year are sitting on the bench, or they're out of the league." Certainly pass receivers are flourishing. The game has become somewhat less grinding and more buoyant. And none too soon.

Swann has flouted conventional wisdom and other forms of repression before. At first he was mortified to be taking dancing lessons, but then he came to like them. He continued taking them all the way through high school and college, and even now, "every once in a while on the field when I'm twisting, jumping, doing a crossover, I think I'm back to dancing."

1979

Thomas Boswell
From Game Day

MIAMI, January 1989 — A generation ago, London subways bore the graffiti "Clapton Is God," as a sort of ultimate inarticulate tribute to that rock guitarist's transcendent riffs. A generation before that, jazz buffs paid the same homage to Charlie Parker, muttering, "Bird is God." What can't be described often gets deified.

Now, it is Jerry Rice who borders on sacrilege. As the San Francisco wideout received his MVP trophy after Sunday's Super Bowl, a 49ers fan who'd sneaked into the ceremony yelled, "Rice is God!"

In the best finish to the best Super Bowl, Rice was the best player. He had more yardage from scrimmage (220) than anyone other than the Redskins' Ricky Sanders (239) last year while saving his best work for the most critical times. "I did okay. . . . I was real lucky," Rice said, in the tradition of Unitas and DiMaggio. "I don't talk a game. I just play it."

And how.

Thomas Boswell

"Rice is not a normal human being. I'm sorry, he's just not," said 49ers veteran Randy Cross. "In the movies, Arnold Schwarzenegger was made in a test tube as the perfect human being. But Jerry Rice is damn near it."

The way Rice moves while a ball is in the air, gliding like a hawk on an air current, and what he does after he grabs that ball, changing direction as suddenly as a snake in water, takes the breath from those who watch him and steals the heart from those who try to defend him.

The range of creative expression in Rice's performance went far beyond the Super Bowl records that he set with 11 catches for 215 yards in the 49ers' 20-16 last-minute victory over the Cincinnati Bengals.

Rice caught a pass entirely with one hand, never touching the ball with the other, as he tapped his feet in bounds. Not bad for a man who, six days ago, sprained his ankle so badly that he was listed as "questionable" for this game.

On another majestic solo, he kept from stepping out of bounds by an inch, then contorted his body and stretched his arm full-length to hook the ball over the goal-line flag for a touchdown. Not bad for a fellow the Bengals said they would intimidate.

Rice shagged posts in traffic, like a 27-yarder in the final minute to set up the winning score, and corners alone, like his touchdown that tied the game, 13-13. He shook deep up the sideline for 30 yards with a defender in his lap. He caught hitches when cornerbacks laid off him in fear and drags just over the middle when linebackers couldn't spin their heads fast enough to find him. He even ran a reverse to open the game.

However, Rice's best catch, and his most symbolic — one that will be played forever on NFL highlights with a basso profundo announcer intoning — came on the 49ers' first play from scrimmage after Stanford Jennings's 93-yard kickoff return had given the Bengals a 13-6 lead. No team ever needed to announce its seriousness more urgently. So Rice went deep.

With Lewis Billups, the Bengal with the big mouth, on his hip, Rice shifted into his marvelous cruise control — the gear in which he seems to run as fast as anybody on the field, but with far more fluid grace and control of his body. Who knows if Rice jumped too soon or whether he simply decided to show a couple of hundred million people that gravity is not quite a universal law.

Billups and others returned to earth. Rice didn't. His fingertip catch for 31 yards lit the fire his teammates needed. It also gave Rice a moment of equality with his childhood hero, Lynn Swann.

"I saw Swann's catch against Dallas in the Super Bowl," said Rice. "The best I ever saw." Now Rice probably owns the second-most-spectacular.

Before this game, the Bengals got cocky, perhaps because of the recurrent bad ankle that has annoyed Rice all season. They said all four of their defensive backs could outsprint him. They said they could beat him up, too.

"My speed is really deceiving," said Rice, his smooth face almost showing annoyance and his big smile fading. "But like I said all week, this is not a track meet...."

1989

Jim Murray
He Adds Perfect Touch

I can't believe No. 8 on the Dallas Cowboys is a real person. It's too perfect.

Look at him: Straight, even white teeth, neatly trimmed blond hair and the level, steady blue-eyed gaze of a lawman on the trail of a varmint in the old West. This guy isn't for real, right? He is Frank Merriwell. Or Hollywood invented him. This is the most perfect casting since Clark Gable as Rhett Butler. Maybe this is Tom Cruise under the helmet and pads.

Troy Aikman as Super Bowl quarterback would get the approval of every film director in town. He has *hero* written all over him. His name should be Frank Faultless or Dick Dauntless. Or maybe Lancelot or Galahad.

Troy Aikman ain't bad.

He just reeks of the Right Stuff. You figure if he weren't a quarterback, he would be an astronaut. In ancient times, he'd be a member of the Knights of the Round Table.

There is not a frivolous thing about him. He is as serious

as a surgeon. He has a nice smile, but he doesn't use it much. He looks like a guy who knows the world is a dangerous place. You never know when a blitz is coming. He wants to be ready.

He is the kind of guy you would want next to you in a foxhole. You can't tell by looking at him whether he is ahead by 10 or behind by 20. Or whether he's got four aces — or a busted flush. You get that same unafraid, unrevealing stare. He makes the Sphinx look emotional. You would hate to play poker with him.

He is not too much fun to play football with. He almost looks bored. But then you expect him to lay down a hand and say, "Are these any good?" and you want to kill him.

If the Dallas Cowboys win the Super Bowl today — and if you don't think so, you get six points — he will be the guy who looks as if he is trying to remember where he left his keys. Don't look for any end zone dances or sidelines shimmies. Look for Aikman. It's only a game, isn't it?

He is 6 feet 4, 220 pounds, the All-American boy, a walking bubble-gum card. He is the NFL's cover boy. That's why it is hard to believe he exists and isn't a product of the sound stages or a lab. You want to say, "Take this back and break a nose. At least, put a scar on the cheek." Girls throw their unmentionables at him, but he remains a bachelor. Anyone else in his position would be working on his third marriage by now. He goes to church on Sunday in the off-season and apologizes because he can't during the season. He is the second coming of Roger Staubach, and if that's so, there might be four more Super Bowls in his resume. He will never be known as "Broadway Troy" or "the Snake" or "Hollywood." Maybe, "Troy Terrific."

But if he only looked the part, he would be merely another pretty face throwing interceptions. Aikman has a chance to go down in history as the best at the position for the Dallas Cowboys since Staubach, who was too good to be true, too.

Aikman is not the only reason the Dallas Cowboys are in the Super Bowl, but he is a main one.

His counterpart today is almost an exact opposite. Jim Kelly smiles all the time, exudes a kind of perpetual Irish charm, is as emotional as the second act of "Carmen," wears his heart on his sleeve and is as convivial as a bartender. Kelly will dance a jig if he wins and probably sing until dawn. The grape will flow. Aikman might celebrate with a pizza-with-everything. And a beer.

Aikman is only now coming into his own. Kelly has been there for some time. If experience is to decide the issue, the outcome should result in the singing of "Kay-ee-double-ell-why!"

But there is something chilling to Aikman's approach, which reminds you of nothing so much as a guy stalking a bear. There's a relentless air about his play. Like him, it's not splashy, simply effective. Ask the San Francisco 49ers. Some think that was the Super Bowl.

He didn't even intend to be a career quarterback. He meant to be a surgeon. He played football to get to medical school. It didn't work. "The time constraints to playing football made getting into the medical field impossible," he says. "The practices, the meetings were too time-consuming. I had to go into something more manageable — management systems first, later sociology."

Medicine might have lost as good a prospect as football gained. The football version of Dr. Aikman conducts his game plans with operating-table precision.

He might never have been the Cowboy's quarterback at all if then-Oklahoma coach Barry Switzer, of all people, had not had a burst of humanitarianism. Aikman, although born in Southern California, was raised in Henryetta, Okla., and recruited by Switzer for his Sooners.

Switzer soon perceived that Aikman, a pure passer, chafed under the restraints of his wishbone system, which put a premium on running. Passing was as afterthought in the wishbone. Magnanimously, Switzer put in a call to UCLA Coach Terry Donahue. Donahue, with his pro pass set, was overjoyed to get this superb technician to run it. Aikman migrated West.

He never made a Rose Bowl, which frustrates him some to this day. But he was good enough — the third-rated passer in NCAA history with more than 5,000 yards and 41 touchdowns in two years — to be the No. 1 pick in the draft.

If he had remained at Oklahoma? Aikman shrugs and says: "There's no doubt (my career) would have turned out drastically different. I would have been a free agent rather than a No. 1 draft choice. But I think I would have caught on somewhere."

Maybe so. But most likely, he would not have been handed the football as quickly as he was at Dallas.

On the other hand, maybe he would have. There is something about Aikman that inspires great trust. You imagine Sergeant York looked like this. He looks as if he is about to clean out Dodge City. If I were Buffalo, I'd try to draw first.

1993

Steve Hubbard
From Great Running Backs

There are only nine men who have ever run for more yards than Barry Sanders, and if he maintains his seven-year pace of 1,453 yards a year, he will surpass Walter Payton as the league's number one runner when he's thirty-two, in the year 2000.

Payton has already conceded. "He's better than I was," Payton said when Sanders was just a rookie. "I was never that good."

Sanders averages 4.9 yards a carry, half a yard better than Payton and Dickerson, better than everyone in the top twenty save Jim Brown. That's probably the best measure of a back's ability and elusiveness. Considering that Sanders has never played with a great line or great team, that fact is even more impressive. Emmitt Smith might have a lion's heart, but there's only one Lion King. Even Dallas coach Barry Switzer admits Sanders is "the most dangerous back in the league" today — and maybe ever.

"He's the best runner that's ever touched the football,"

Fontes said. "If anybody thinks he isn't, then they're not watching football."

Gale Sayers said that Sanders is the only back today who reminds him of himself. Steve Sabol said, "You could put him in a phone booth with someone else and it'd be ten minutes before the other guy could touch him." Green Bay coach Mike Holmgren said that Sanders is "quicker than any man I've ever seen."

Detroit assistant head coach Dave Levy, who coached O.J., said that Sanders has the best balance he's ever seen. Ex-Vikings coach Jerry Burns says that Sanders has Earl Campbell's leg strength and is so slippery, that he must wear silicone spray on his jersey. The officials checked; he doesn't. Seattle safety Eugene Robinson said that Sanders combines Barry Foster's power and Smith's elusiveness. "Oh boy, can he make you miss."

Just ask Patriot safety Harlon Barnett. Sanders turned him around on one play. Or ask the Tampa Bay Buccaneers. One of their defensive men yanked off his shoe 7 yards downfield, but none could tackle him until 78 yards later.

Sanders burst into the nation's consciousness in 1988. After being Thurman Thomas' backup for two years at Oklahoma State, he set thirteen NCAA records with 2,628 rushing yards and 39 touchdowns. Still, when he chose to turn pro early, the NFL scouts had two worries. First, the Heisman Trophy winner was only five-feet eight-inches tall. Second, the Dallas Cowboys and Green Bay Packers had committed the first two picks to Troy Aikman and Tony Mandarich, and with the third pick, Detroit was considering Barry Sanders, Deion Sanders, and Tim Worley. However, when a bunch of clubs finally trekked out to Stillwater, Oklahoma to watch Sanders work out, the debate soon ended.

He covered 40 yards in 4.27 seconds; covered 40, 41,

and 42 inches in his vertical jumps; and made 11 feet from a standing broad jump.

Fontes lit a cigar like a proud new papa, unable to conceal his grin. "My running back won't be doing anything else today," he told the other scouts. "Thank you for coming."

"Everybody thought I was kidding," Fontes later recalled. "I wasn't."

Still, the Lions didn't sign Sanders until just two days before the opener. He had time to learn just four plays, only one well. No practice? No matter. On his first carry he ran for 18 yards and on his fourth carry he scored a touchdown. On his fifth carry he gained 26 yards, and by the end of the quarter — after 9 carries — he had gained 71 yards.

In Sanders' next game, six-foot-four-inch, 235-pound All-Pro Carl Banks nailed him dead-on. But Sanders broke the tackle. On the following Sunday, Sanders had his first 100-yard game by halftime, versus the Bears. Three games into Sanders' pro career, Mike Ditka surrendered. Ditka had coached or played with Payton, Sayers, and Tony Dorsett. "Barry Sanders," he said, "is as fine a running back as I've ever seen."

1996

An excerpt from Great Running Backs, *New York, 1996, Michael Friedman Publishing Group, Inc.*

Dick Wimmer

Pro Football's Greatest All-Around Player

Frank Gifford? Charlie Trippi? Otto Graham? Paul Hornung? How about Orban (Spec) Sanders? Who? say my colleagues. Who? say my friends. Who? say my two sons. They and their '90s generation have never even heard of Spec Sanders. Well, having just talked to the good ol' boy himself, I'm happy to report that he is alive and well and still living in Lawton, Oklahoma at the vibrant age of seventy-nine.

But who was Spec Sanders? And what did he accomplish?

After two years of junior college football in Cameron, Oklahoma, he transferred to the University of Texas in 1940, but played in the shadow of Pete Layden as a 6-1, 197 pound tailback. He spent the war years, 1942-1945, as a Navy lieutenant, mainly in the South Pacific, and sharpened his football skills against top caliber Pre-Flight competition, including one season in the same backfield with Otto Graham.

When he finally arrived on the pro scene after the war,

he was twenty-seven, mentally mature and at his physical peak. He was signed in 1946 by the New York Yankees of the newly formed All-America Football Conference. This rival to the NFL only lasted through 1949, but it produced the Cleveland Browns, Baltimore Colts, and San Francisco 49ers, and such stars as Graham, Marion Motley, "Crazylegs" Hirsch, Joe Perry, Frankie Albert, and Y.A. Tittle. It was the first league to play a 14-game regular season schedule, the first to travel by air (the NFL still rode trains), and during its four years of existence outdrew the NFL in average attendance.

Spec led the AAFC in rushing his rookie year and made all-league halfback, despite playing both ways and alternating at tailback with Ace Parker, now in the Hall of Fame. He caught 17 passes, completed 33, returned punts and kickoffs (a 30.4 average), and did his team's punting. The Yankees won the Eastern Division, but lost to the Cleveland Browns before 70,000 in the championship game.

But the best was yet to come. In 1947, Spec completed the greatest all-around season in pro football history. He took over sole possession of tailback in the Yankees' single-wing attack, played safety on defense, as well as starring once more on specialty teams and doing the punting. He led the league again in rushing with the then unbelievable total of 1432 yards gained and a 6.2 average per carry, scored a league-high 18 touchdowns on the ground, threw for 1442 yards, completing 54.4% of his passes for 14 touchdowns, averaged 27.3 yards per punt return, 27 yards per kickoff return (including one for 103 yards), led his club in interceptions, and averaged 42.1 per punt, his longest traveling 84 yards.

Buddy Young, his outstanding running mate and later director of Player Relations in Commissioner Pete Rozelle's office, said Spec's long, gliding gait was deceptive. "No one took the trouble to measure his stride, but you'd probably have found it was as long as the great Gale Sayers. I've always considered Spec part of a select group of runners like Hugh McElhenny, George Taliaferro, Marion Motley, Jimmy Brown, Lenny Moore, and Sayers."

Spec's encore season produced 759 yards rushing (105 short of Motely's league-leading total) and a 4.5 yard average, 78 pass completions, and a 40.6 yard punting average.

He sat out the entire '49 season due to a knee operation. And in 1950, the AAFC merged with the NFL, the Browns, 49ers, and Colts joining the older league.

The Yankees were renamed the New York Yanks and switched to a T-formation attack. Spec told his coach, Red Strader, that though willing to play offense — his knee was fine, he'd rather play safety. So that season, he led the league with 13 interceptions, a new record, and was named all-pro as a defensive back. He also punted 71 times with a 42.3 yard average.

He retired the next year. "I was still in pretty good shape," Spec says, "but I figured I'd walk away while I was all together."

In 1952, he went into the dry cleaning business in Lawton, Oklahoma, and sold his company in 1976. Today he continues to play golf four times a week, and every morning does 50 push-ups, 50 toe-touches, and 50 leg-lifts.

How good does he think he was? Spec pauses a moment, then replies, "Oh, I think I did as well as a lot of those boys."

The NFL has never recognized AAFC records, and Spec Sanders, as of this morning, is still not in the Hall of Fame.

1997

Pat Conroy

From The Prince of Tides

The team, forty of us, fully dressed, moved through the long corridor that led from the locker room to the conference room. Our spikes dragged along the cement and we sounded like the approach of bison crossing a plain of flint. Hanging bulbs illuminated our white jerseys; huge shadows cast by the strange light danced off the wall as we walked in the superhuman unearthly disguise of our violent sport.

We entered the conference room and sat down unhurriedly in folding chairs. Outside, we could hear the crowd humming in the long dusk. The pep band played a medley of fight songs. Then we heard Caesar roar, and with Luke leading the cheers, we roared back. Then the coach began to speak.

"Tonight, I'm gonna learn and the town's gonna learn who my hitters are. All you've proved so far is that you know how to put on pads and get dates to the sock hop after the game, but until I see you in action, I won't know if you're hitters or not. Real hitters. Now a real hitter is a headhunter who puts his head in the chest of his opponent and ain't happy if his opponent is still breathing after the play. A real hitter doesn't know what fear is except when he sees it in the eyes of a ball carrier he's about to split in half. A real hitter loves pain, loves the screaming and the sweating and the brawling and the hatred of life down in the trenches. He likes to be at the spot where the blood flows and teeth get kicked out. That's what this sport's all about, men. It's war, pure and simple. Now tonight, you go out there and kick butt all over that field. If something moves, hit it. If something breathes, hit it. And if something has tits, f—k it."

There was some laughter in the room but not much. This was the fourth year in a row Coach Sams had delivered the exact same pregame speech and even the obligatory joke was the same. He always talked about football as if he were in the hysterical final stages of rabies.

"Now do I have me some hitters?" he screamed, veins throbbing along his temple.

"Yes, sir," we screamed back.

"Do I have some f——g hitters?"

"Yes, sir."

"Do I have me some g—damn headhunters?"

"Yes, sir."

"Am I going to see blood?"

"Yes, sir."

"Am I going to see their guts hanging off your helmets?"

"Yes, sir," we happy hitters cried aloud.

"Let us pray," he said.

He led the team in the recitation of the Lord's Prayer.

Then he turned the floor over to Luke and he left the room and waited for the team outside.

Luke rose, massive in his pads. He surveyed the room.

THE GRIDIRON GAME

At two hundred and forty pounds, Luke was one of the largest men in Colleton County and certainly the strongest. His presence soothed; his calmness made us calm.

"You young kids on the team," Luke began, "don't worry too much about Coach Sams. He just likes to talk it up. It doesn't mean all that much. And he forgot to tell you something. Forgot to tell all of us something. The reason we play this game is to have fun. That's the long and short of it. We go out to have a good time, to block and tackle and run the best we can, and to work together as a team. I want to talk about the team in a very specific way. We should have talked about it since the season began. We need to talk about Benji."

There was a stirring of discontent throughout the room and everyone looked around to find the black boy. He was sitting alone in the last chair in the room. He faced the eyes of his teammates with the same silent, resolute dignity with which he navigated the halls of the school. He looked impassively at Luke.

"Now none of us wanted Benji to come to our school. But he did. We didn't want him to come out for our team, either. But he did. At practice we went after him with everything we had. We gang-tackled him, punched him, beat up on him, tried to hurt him — anything we could to make him quit. I did it, too. He took everything we dished out. And now, I want you to know, Benji, that you're a member of this football team, and I'm proud that you're on it. I think you've made it a hell of lot better team than it would have been, and I'll beat the s—t out of anyone here tonight who thinks any different. Benji, come on up here and sit in the first row."

Benji hesitated and I could hear the room breathing again. He got up and walked down the center aisle with every eye of every boy riveted upon him, his eyes never leaving Luke's.

"Now tonight, North Charleston is going to go after Benji. They're gonna call you nigger and every other thing, Benji, and there's nothing we can do to stop it. But I want all the rest of you to know that Benji ain't no nigger when we go out that door. Benji's a teammate. And there ain't no word more beautiful to me than teammate. He ain't no nigger now and he ain't gonna be one for the rest of the year. He's a Tiger from Colleton High just like the rest of us. And if they get on him, we get on them. That's the way I see it. And Benji, I hope I didn't embarrass you by all this, but I don't see how it can't be said. I had to get it out. Does anyone here disagree with me?"

There was the sound of the band, the crowd, the nervous tapping of cleats on the floor, but no voices of dissent.

"Tom, do you have anything to say to the team?"

I rose, turned to my teammates, and said in a breathless excited voice: "Let's win."

❧

I carry with me always the memories of my time as an athlete and those life-changing, exultant nights when I took to the measured fields and tested my strength and swiftness and character against that of other boys. I lived for the subsidies and praise of ingathered crowds, the rousing music of bands, the pixilation of cheerleaders high-kicking to the rhythm of drums, chanting out the urgent banalities of the sport with both eroticism and religious conviction. The sight of the opposing team, black-helmeted and serious, sent a shiver of delectating pleasure down my spine. I listened to the happy cadences of their vigorous warming-up like a blind man leaning toward a window full of birds. Games, games, games, I sang, as my brother and I led our team in calisthenics. On the green field of Colleton, I would taste immortality for the first and last time in my life. I could smell the salt air coming off the river, the piquant tang of that endless acreage of familiar tides spiced with a hint of crops mellowing on sea islands. My senses deepened, ignited, and I was fully alive, like something not quite human staring into the eyes of God on the first day of Eden. I could feel the breath of God running like light through my bloodstream. I shouted, I exhorted my teammates, I danced in the lean, honed grandeur of being a boy, gifted in his chosen game, as the referee's whistle pierced the air and Luke and I walked to the center of the field for the toss of the coin. The referee flipped a silver dollar high in the air and Luke called "heads" and heads it was. We elected to receive.

And on this night, I raised my fist in a gesture of concordance with Benji Washington as he and I took our positions as deep backs and awaited the opening kickoff from the North Charleston High Blue Devils. I watched their kicker approach the ball, saw their team break and flow and the ball spinning high through the lights, and heard myself yell, "You take it, Benji."

He caught it in the end zone and sprinted to the thirty-five before he was hit and hit hard by two North Charleston players. He vanished beneath a pile of blue jerseys. The North Charleston team, unhinged, frenzied, out of control, leapt to their feet, screaming at Benji. Five hundred fans from North Charleston had traveled south for the game, and a chant of "Nigger, nigger, nigger" rose up from the visitors' side of the field.

"We're going to kill you, nigger," their safety, number twenty-eight, shouted at Benji, who rose from the ground slowly.

They rushed up to Benji and followed him almost to the

huddle in a profane, violent pack.

"Nigger. Nigger. F——g nigger," they screamed at him.

They were still screaming when I called the first play of the season. My teammates were shaken. Benji was in a state of shock.

As we lined up, the North Charleston line went down in tandem, screaming, "Kill the nigger." As I bent down over the center, their safety yelled at me, "Give me the g—damn coon."

I lifted up, pointed my finger at the safety, and shouted pleasantly, "F—k you, c—k sucker."

The whistle blew and the head linesman signaled a fifteen-yard penalty against us for unsportsmanlike conduct. He said the words unsportmanlike conduct with a nasal drawl that made him sound like an off-duty Klansman. I would find no Supreme Court justices among the referees of rural South Carolina.

"Hey, ref," I said, "how about making them stop yelling at number forty-four?"

"I don't hear them yelling at anyone," the referee said.

"Then you must not have heard me say 'F—k you, c—k sucker' to that zit-faced back."

The whistle blew a second time and the referee marked off half the distance to the goal line. So far, my brilliant quarterbacking had lost us twenty-five yards and I had yet to receive a snap from center.

"Shut up and play ball," the referee ordered.

"Come and get it, nigger," their safety yelled across to Benji. "I'm gonna kick your nuts in, nigger. Gonna kill us a nigger tonight. Gonna eat nigger meat."

The North Charleston crowd maintained the cry of "nigger" and it grew louder. The Colleton fans were silent and watchful. I saw Benji's parents sitting alone at the top

THE GRIDIRON GAME

of the bleachers. His mother's face had turned away from the field. His father watched stoically and I knew where Benji's impassive, regal bearing originated.

I called time out.

My teammates were cringing in the huddle, like these scurvy hounds who live off garbage at county landfill projects. I, ever the prescient quarterback, recognized that my team had not quite jelled. Their lethargy matched my rising fury. I wanted to eat a goal post or beat their faces in. From down field, along the track, I saw the cage where Caesar slept, kindly untutored in the malevolence of the language.

I knelt and spoke to my team: "Okay, men. It's me, the quarterback. The f——g golden boy. Ol' Tom Wingo is going to give a pep talk."

"Nigger, nigger, nigger." The cry echoed off the schoolhouse wall as the citizens of Colleton watched in eerie silence.

"Now I want you to loosen up. Benji, I know this is tough on you. It's tough on all of us. It's scary. But before we show them that you're the fastest black-assed bastard in the world, we're going to take care of a little business. Now you guys are acting dead. I want a little life. I want some noise."

A small cheer, which would not do, rose up from the team.

"Luke," I said, taking my huge brother by the shoulder pads and slapping the side of his helmet with an open palm. "Luke, make Caesar roar."

"What?"

"Make Caesar roar," I ordered again.

Luke walked away from the huddle toward the North Charleston team and looked at the cage, which was parked in darkness. He walked almost to the line of scrimmage, looked far down the field, and screamed out over the noise of the chant to the Wingo family tiger, who, bored by the lights and football, slept amidst fish bones and the remnants of chicken necks until he heard the powerful strained voice of the human being he loved best, calling, "Roar, Caesar, roar."

Caesar came to his cage's bars, not as pet, not as joke, not as mascot, but as Bengal tiger, and he roared out a greeting of affirmation and constancy to the largest right tackle in the state.

Luke answered him with a human affectionate roar of his own.

Caesar roared again and it crossed that football field like a plane, drowning out the puny chant of "nigger," dwarfing the voice of crowds, crossed the fifty-yard line, swept into our ears, broke through the parking lot, hit the brick wall off the gymnasium, and echoed back as if a second great cat had been born behind us. Caesar answered his own echo and I shouted at my teammates, "Now, motherf——s, gutless shits, babies. Answer back. Answer Caesar."

Together, my teammates roared like tigers at the tiger. Again and again, they roared, and Caesar, no rookie under the lights, who had been born to perform and preserved the instinct for the center ring, responded with the magnificent feral voice that had originated in the steaming forests of India. Caesar, whose parents had awakened Hindu tribes at night and stirred the adrenaline of elephants, delivered a message to the soul of my team. Then the Colleton crowd ignited, remembering the spirit of the game, and the tiger moved through their ranks and the field trembled with their roaring.

I raced to the sidelines and shouted at Mr. Chappel, the band director, to strike up "Dixie." When that band broke into "Dixie," Caesar went wild. I watched the North Charleston team stare at the full-grown Bengal tiger snarling, crazed, attacking the bars of his cage, his forelegs swinging outside the bars, claws fully extended: a study in the limits of wildness. Luke charged up to me furiously.

"Why did you do that, Tom?" he said. "You know that song upsets Caesar."

"He's looking for one of those f——g seals," I said, swollen with pride. "Enjoy this, Luke. This is the greatest timeout in the history of football." I walked toward the North Charleston team, who watched transfixed as their fans grew silent and baffled.

"Hey, boys," I yelled above the din, "piss me off again and I'm gonna let that tiger loose on the field."

The whistle blew and we were penalized for delaying the game.

Then we huddled and something magic had happened. In the eyes of my teammates, I saw that sacred gleam of oneness, of solidarity, of brotherhood, which is the most glorious thing in the kingdom of sport. It lives in the heart but is secreted through the eyes. I saw the coming together, the making of the team.

"Nigger, nigger. Roar, roar." The sounds enveloped us.

I said, "The first offensive play of the season for the Colleton Tigers is this: Quarterback sneak. Only no one block for me. While those jerks are creaming my ass I want every single person on this team except Benji to go after that creep of a safety. I'm just going to run around a little in the backfield and give you time to get him."

"Nigger, nigger. Roar, roar," said the crowds.

When I received the snap, I did a small inelegant softshoe toward a slight opening off left guard when five hundred pounds of boyflesh and leather hit me at the same time and drove me into the ground, my face crushed into the grass and lime of our own five-yard line. The whistle blew and when I got up I could see their safety lying on his back, clutching his face and knee. Our team was assessed another fifteen-yard penalty for unnecessary roughness and the referee walked off half the distance of the goal line. I had skillfully engineered this retreat, which left us thirty-two yards behind our original scrimmage line. But I watched with pleasure as they carried the safety out of the game, bleeding, as Luke happily described it, from every orifice in his body.

"The nigger's gonna pay for that," one of their linebackers shouted.

In the huddle, I knelt and said, "Good boys. Good boys. I like it when you listen to Uncle Tom. Now, on the next play we're gonna try to score a touchdown."

"Here comes Benji," Luke crowed.

"Not yet," I said. "The master strategist ain't using Benji yet. But he'll be the decoy. I'm sending you right up the middle, Benji. I'm going to tell them you're getting the ball and gonna show them the hole you'll be coming through."

"Jesus," Benji said.

"That's stupid, Tom," Luke said.

"But I ain't gonna give you the ball. I'm bootlegging it around left end. Get me some blockers down field. On two. Break."

As I approached the line, before I put my hands beneath Milledge Morris's redolent behind, I walked toward that monotonous chant of "nigger" again. I said aloud to the whole North Charleston team: "You want the nigger? I'm gonna send him through this hole right here." I pointed to the hole between the center and left guard. "And none of you have the nuts to stop him."

I watched their linebacker shift and the defensive backs

shift a few steps toward the hole as the cadence rolled off my tongue.

"Set, fourteen, thirty-five, two."

I came up with the ball held low, heard the helmets and pads of the linemen break out behind me, crouched low and stuck the ball into Benji's stomach as he shot past, watched him drive toward the hole, then pulled the ball slickly out as he disappeared into the arms of the white South.

With the ball on my hip, I looked back, pretending to slow up as I saw the pile of blue jerseys pulling Benji to the earth. Then I hit the corner and shot down those sidelines right past those North Charleston fans who suddenly remembered there were white boys on the Colleton team, too. At the twenty, Luke joined me and we both ran with our eye on the defensive back with a talent for not believing liars. He moved to cut me off at the sidelines and I faked to my right as if I were reversing my field. He slowed and straightened and Luke half killed him with a cross-body block as I leapt over both of them without breaking stride and moved into the clear at our own twenty-five-yard line.

I have kept my father's film of that game and have watched that ninety-seven-yard dash up the sidelines a hundred times and will watch it a hundred times again before I die. I watch the boy I once was and marvel at his speed as I observe his progress in the grainy, surreal image of the film and run my hand through thinning hair. I try to recapture that moment when I ran toward the end zone, entering into my own territory, now pursued vainly by frantic boys in blue jerseys. The crowd took possession of me at the fifty-yard line; I felt it in my legs, that dreaming hum of human voices urging me toward speed, toward the highest thresholds of those ecstatic running days. I ran as a Colleton boy who had brought his town to its feet, and there is nothing happier on earth than a running boy, nothing so innocent or untouched. I was gifted and young, uncatchable as I sprinted down the sidelines followed by a referee I left in the dust. Swift and dazzling through the light I ran, past the eyes of my screaming father, who followed my progress through a glass aperture, past my twin sister leaping and twisting on the sidelines, cherishing the moment because she cherished me, past my mother, whose beauty could not disguise her shame at who she was and what she had come from. But at this moment — mythic and elegiac — she was the mother of Tom Wingo and had given the world those legs and that speed as a gift, and I crossed the forty and in the next second the thirty, sprinting past my life as a boy toward the end zone. But as I watch this film, I often think that the boy did not know what he was really running toward, that it was not the end zone which awaited him. Somewhere in that ten-second dash the running boy turned to metaphor and the older man could see it where the boy could not. He would be good at running, always good at it, and he would always run away from the things that hurt him, from the people who loved him, and from the friends empowered to save him. But where do we run when there are no crowds, no lights, no end zones? Where does a man run? the coach said, studying the films of himself as a boy. Where can a man run when he has lost the excuse of games? Where can a man run or where can he hide when he looks behind him and sees that he is only pursued by himself?

I crossed the end zone and threw the ball fifty feet straight into the air. I threw myself down and kissed the grass. I ran to Caesar's cage and rattled the bars. "Cheer, you yellow son of a bitch." Imperially, he ignored me.

Then Luke caught me up in his arms, lifted me off the

THE GRIDIRON GAME

ground, and spun me around and around. Luke and I, at last, had our waltz.

We kicked off and I knew from the way we swarmed all over the ball carrier that this was our night. On their first play from scrimmage, Luke met their fullback head on and drove him back five yards into the grass. The whole right side of the line was in on the tackle when they tried a power sweep around the end. Luke blitzed and threw the quarterback for a seven-yard loss on the third down. Our whole team was on fire and we pounded each other on the shoulder pads and helmets, embraced each other after every play, and screamed encouragement to the lineman who made the first hit. There were unquenchable titanic fires loose on that field, a sense of recognition and payoff and destiny.

The punter kicked a fifty-yard punt that went out of bounds on the fifty-yard line. Now I planned to set Benji loose. When I was scoring the touchdown Benji was at the bottom of the pile getting his eyes thumbed, his leg bit, and his dander up.

"Benji, we're going to teach these poor crackers about the merits of Brown versus the Board of Education. Tackle slot right on four. Break."

I almost felt a bit sorry for the kid who played across the line from Luke. At the beginning of the game he would be a nice strapping healthy kid, and at game's end he would be a paraplegic for at least a day. With Luke's remarkable size and grace it was no accident that he discovered a natural affinity for tigers.

As I approached the line, the word nigger had disappeared for a time from the vocabulary of the North Charleston Blue Devils.

I handed off to Benji Washington, the first time a white boy had ever handed the ball to a black boy in my part of the world. He broke off tackle (Luke had done something like eat the boy in front of him), spun off a linebacker who cracked into him, shot off the end who tried to arm-tackle him, then in a series of astonishing moves of such swiftness and deception, he danced into their backfield, wiggling, frenetic, untouchable, and cut suddenly against the flow, reversing his field, then dashing past the right defensive back to the sidelines, then cutting hard, he raced the whole North Charleston team for the end zone. Three players had shots at him but all three misjudged his speed. As we slowfooted boys followed him to the goal line, we had scored our second touchdown in less than two minutes. I could feel the ambivalence of the Colleton crowd, and for a moment, there was nothing but polite stunned applause. This was a white crowd, southern to the bone, mired in all the inhumane traditions of our time, and something in them wanted Benji to fail, even if it meant the team had to fail. Some of them probably even wanted Benji to die. But somewhere in that seven-second dash, resistance to integration weakened just a tiny bit in Colleton. And every time Benji Washington carried the ball that night, the southerners' awesome love of sport won out over the bruised history that had brought the fastest human being in the American South into our backfield. When the team surrounded Benji, half killing him with their punches and slaps, he said to Luke, "God, these white boys are slow."

"Naw," Luke answered, "you were just scared they'd catch you."

I learned that night that with Benji Washington in the backfield I was a much better quarterback than I was meant to be. I sent him through the line or around end thirty times that night. I watched him break up the middle for five, sweep end for twenty-five, slant off tackle for eleven. In the third

THE GRIDIRON GAME

quarter, I sprinted to my right on an option play, watched the defensive end overcommit himself as I faked a lateral to Benji. I darted through the hole over left tackle and angled toward the sideline until I was hit by the outside linebacker. As I fell, I flipped the ball to Benji who caught it and in a straight pure celebration of speed raced down the sidelines for eighty yards, untouched by human hands.

In the fourth quarter North Charleston rallied for two touchdowns, but they were hard-earned, furiously contested scores. Both times they scored on long grueling marches down field and both times their fullback broke over from the one-yard line after being repulsed twice before. With the clock winding down and with us leading 42-14, our band played "The Tennessee Waltz" and as North Charleston broke from their huddle, they found us dancing helmet to helmet at the line of scrimmage with the crowd singing the words in the bleachers.

Then the whistle blew, ending the game, and our town was on us. They burst onto the field and we walked back to the locker room crushed and pummeled by a thousand students and fans. Savannah found me and kissed me on the lips, laughing when I blushed. Luke tackled me from behind and wrestled me on the grass. Three North Charleston linemen fought their way through the crowd and shook Benji's hand. Their middle linebacker apologized for calling him a nigger. Caesar began roaring again and was joined by the crowd. My father filmed it all. My mother jumped up into Luke's arms and he carried her like a bride all the way to the locker room, her arms wrapped around his neck, telling him how wonderful she thought he was, how proud she was.

In the locker room, the team threw Coach Sams into the showers fully clothed. Oscar Woodhead and Chuck

Richards picked up Benji and carried him almost reverently to the shower room, where he was baptized in the ritual waters of victory. Luke and I were lifted and carried, too, until the whole team, ecstatic and triumphant, stood dripping and screaming on the tiles as photographers snapped pictures and our fathers lit cigarettes and discussed the game outside the locker room.

1986

Ed Linn

Glenn Davis and Doc Blanchard

In 1944, Davis and Blanchard were almost immediately put in the same backfield. Blaik's material was so rich that he was able to anticipate the two-platoon system, not with offensive and defensive units, but with two separate two-way teams. The starting backfield had Doug Kenna, Max Minor, Dale Hall and Bobby Dobbs. The plebe backfield had Blanchard, Davis and Dean Sensanbaugher plus Captain Tom Lombardo. Glenn, who had worn a fullback's number his first year (34), was given a halfback's number, 41. Blanchard was given number 35. For the next three years, 35 and 41 would be the numbers to look for when the Army team was on the field.

The Big Rabble — as the team is known at the Point — rambled. Blaik always started his veteran backfield, with the plebes coming on late in the first quarter or at the start of the second. It really wasn't an athletic contest when the barefoot college boys of 1944 — a smattering of V-12s, pre-drafts and rejects — met Army's pair of powerhouses; it was cruel and unusual punishment. In Doc Blanchard they reaped the whirlwind, in Junior Davis they clutched at a gust of wind. Doc stunned them and Junior dazzled them.

Army beat North Carolina, 6-0, Brown 59-7, Pittsburgh 62-7, and only Blaik's sense of compassion kept the scores as low as that.

Playing sometimes little more than a quarter, and rarely more than a half, Davis scored three touchdowns against major opponents North Carolina, Brown, Notre Dame, Villanova and Pennsylvania.

After Army had shellacked Notre Dame, 59-0, racking up more points than they had scored against the Irish in the fifteen previous years combined, Allison Danzig of the New York Times wrote: "Twenty years after the Four Horsemen rode to lasting fame, the proud pennants of Notre Dame were ripped to tatters and trampled under the thundering caissons of Army yesterday in the worst disaster the Fighting Irish have suffered on a football field."

Blanchard didn't score, but his ferocious play brought forth the usual expressions of awe and wonder. Running interference for Kenna on a punt, he hit "Tree" Adams, Notre Dame's 6-foot, 7-inch tackle, with a blind-angle block that knocked him, quite literally, for a loop. Adams went up in the air, turned a complete somersault and landed on the back of his neck.

Comment on Doc started at superlatives and went on up to sublime. Clark Shaughnessy said: "Blanchard is the greatest fullback I have ever seen." (And Shaughnessy had coached Bronko Nagurski and Norm Standlee.)

Jack Lavelle said: "Blanchard is the greatest football player I have ever seen."

Notre Dame coach Ed McKeever wired home the message: "Have just seen Superman in the flesh. He wears No.

THE GRIDIRON GAME

35 and goes by the name of Blanchard."

The big game was still Navy. The Middies had done a little scrounging around in the marketplace themselves, and they had a sea-worthy football squad. Because of travel limitations, the game was originally supposed to be played at Annapolis, with half the Middies detailed to cheer for Army. At the last minute, the brass got so excited about the game that they put it into Baltimore's Municipal Stadium. Admission was restricted to purchasers of War Bonds residing within a ten-mile radius of the city and 66,639 people, some of whom may have lived 11 miles from the city, showed up.

It was a ball game worth traveling ten miles to see. At the end of three quarters, Army was leading, 9-7, when Davis intercepted a pass on his own 35 and swung on down to the 48.

They gave the ball to Blanchard, and Little Doc did his father proud. They gave it to him for 25 around right end, then they gave it to him for 3 over left tackle. Davis got 3 around right end, then Doc went up the middle for 5 yards and a first down on the 21. Max Minor made a yard, and then it was all Doc again. It was Blanchard for 3, Blanchard for 4, Blanchard for 3 more and a first down on the 10. So they gave it to Blanchard once more and he smashed inside left guard and hit the end zone standing up.

("This is the only man," Herman Hickman said afterwards, "who runs his own interference.")

The next time Army got the ball, it was Glenn's turn. Blaik had designed a weak-side play for him called "The California Special." The ball came to him on a direct shovel from Lombardo, and Glenn cut inside the end and swung to the sideline where, with that extraordinary ability to rev his speed up notch by notch ("Davis' unlimited gearshifts,"

Blaik called it), he shot by every man who had a crack at him. The final score was 23-7.

At the end of the season, Davis was the country's leading scorer with 20 touchdowns; his average per carry was a fantastic 12.4 yards. Blanchard had 9 touchdowns and a 7.1 per-carry average. Both were, of course, almost unanimous All-America choices.

Davis was given the Maxwell Club Trophy, the Walter Camp Award and the Helms Foundation Award. Glenn and Doc ran second and third behind Ohio State's Les Horvath in the voting for the Heisman Trophy.

The following year, in 1945, Army may have had the greatest college team ever assembled. The ends were Barney Poole and Hank Foldberg, the tackles were Tex Coulter and Al Nemetz, the guards captain Johnny Green and Art Gerometta, the center Ug Fuson. Joining Davis and Blanchard in the backfield were Arnold Tucker, up from third string, and Shorty McWilliams, up from Mississippi State.

With Tucker's adept passing forcing the opposition to worry about its anti-aircraft as well as its flanks and center, Blaik had a perfectly balanced attack. It crushed Wake Forest, 54-0, Michigan 27-7, Duke, 48-13, Villanova, 54-0, Notre Dame, 48-0, Pennsylvania, 61-0, and Navy, 32-13.

In the first half of the Notre Dame game, Glenn scored three times and Doc twice. Then Blaik, as was his custom, retired them for the afternoon. "Heck, Colonel," Davis said, throwing away his helmet in disgust, "I want to play football and you're not giving me a chance."

Blanchard scored twice in the first quarter against Navy and Davis went 49 yards for a third. For sheer, unbridled power, Doc's second score was frightening. Clyde (Smackover) Scott, whom Navy had picked up from Arkansas (the university, not the battleship), had a head-on shot at him in an open field. Doc just ran over him.

Blanchard had 19 touchdowns in the year; Davis had 18. It was Doc's year, however. He beat Glenn out for the Heisman Trophy, and he won both the Maxwell Cup and the Walter Camp Trophy. More than that, he became the first football player ever to win the AAU's Sullivan Award as the outstanding amateur athlete in the country.

In 1946, the brave old Army team began to come apart. Rip Rowan joined Blanchard, Davis and Tucker in the backfield, but the heart of the line — Green, Nemetz and Coulter — had left. In the opening game, against Villanova, Blanchard twisted away from a tackler and, before he could pick up speed again, Penn's 200-pound end, Francis Kane, hit him around the shoulders. Doc's foot sunk into the wet ground. The knee, instead of bending in as he fell, bent out — like a door being yanked against the hinge. Two different sets of ligaments were torn. Normally, such an injury would be expected to put a man out for the season. Apparently, however, Doc's fantastic calf and thigh development acted as a shock absorber, for he came back to face Michigan after missing only two games. He wasn't the same Blanchard — he didn't kick anymore and he didn't scrimmage — but he was back.

The Michigan game was a day of reckoning. The men were beginning to stream home from the wars, and, more important perhaps, fewer boys were being drafted. Michigan, under Fritz Crisler, was coming fast. Bob Chappuis, Bump Elliot, Jack Weisenburger and Paul White were in the backfield; Len Ford and Bob Mann were at the ends. (Throughout the era of Blanchard and Davis, there had always been the feeling, even on the part of the most faithful rooter, that the true ability of the Army team could never accurately be gauged, since the opposition was so underprivileged.) On the fourth play of the game, Tucker suffered a shoulder separation plus a sprained elbow and a wrist on his passing arm. He kept the injury to himself and stayed in the game, but with Tucker and Blanchard both under anesthetic, the wheel swung around and pointed to Junior. With Army trailing, 7-0, he took the ball on Michigan's 41, snuck through guard and ran right into a small patrol of tacklers. Junior didn't surrender. He shook off three successive tacklers as he cut to his right, and suddenly and astonishingly, he was running free down the sidelines. At the 15-yard line, he was blocked in against the sideline by Paul White, but there never was a ball carrier harder to build a fence around than Glenn Davis. In a typical Davis maneuver, he faked in toward the middle of the field and, in almost the same split second, accelerated his speed and squeezed through on the sideline. White had moved with him on the fake, and that was all the help Glenn needed.

With the half coming to a close, Tucker called a pass play from the Michigan 23, on fourth and 18. The left side of the Michigan line broke through and roughed Davis up just as he was taking Tucker's hand-off. The ball squirted loose and bounced away. Two Michigan lineman dived for it and missed. Davis, running back and to his right, grabbed it on a big hop and, in the same motion, jumped turned and threw to the right corner of the end zone. He couldn't have dropped it better if he had been standing there on a ladder. Bob Folsom, a second-string end, made the catch, with a little jump off his full stride. Army was ahead, but not for long. Michigan took the second-half kickoff and marched for the tying score.

In the fourth quarter, Doc Blanchard, who had been pushed around all afternoon, came to life. He leaped high in the air at midfield to pluck a Davis pass away from a pack of drooling wolverines. He began to get that short yardage through the line. With the ball on the 18, Mr. Inside and Mr. Outside switched roles. Glenn slammed up the middle for 3, Blanchard went wide for 8. From the 7-yard line, Doc went around left end and headed for the corner. He was hit twice on the 3-yard line, but, bad leg or no, he carried both tacklers into the end zone. Final score: Army 20, Michigan, 13.

Army lost the battle of statistics, but won the game, It was the big answer on Blanchard and Davis. The line didn't do it for them, the blocking didn't do it for them. They did it themselves. Davis had run 105 yards and completed seven out of eight passes for 168 yards. It was, Red Blaik believes, Glenn's greatest game.

Notre Dame, with Frank Leahy and Johnny Lujack back from the wars, finally stopped them. No game ever provoked more interest. "If Yankee Stadium had a million seats," athletic director Biff Jones said, "we would still fill it for this game." Unfortunately, it turned out to be a dull game — a scoreless tie. Army's string of twenty-five successive victories was broken.

In the Navy game, Blanchard looked like his old armor-clad self for the first time since his injury. It was just as well that he did. He exploded 53 yards for one touchdown, and caught a Davis pass — on a stop-start pattern — for another. Davis had scored earlier on a dazzling 14-yard run. But Navy, given absolutely no chance to extend Army, took complete charge of the second half and brought the score to 21-18. With a minute and a half to go, they had the ball on the Army 3, and it seemed almost certain that the fabulous careers of Davis and Blanchard would end on a stunning note of defeat. Navy had three cracks at the winning touchdown, but Army held. In three years, the Blanchard-Davis clubs had won 27 games, and tied one. They had never known defeat.

1964

Ira Berkow
≥&
Riggins and Life Without Blockers

He is still asked on the streets, "Hey Riggo, how's Sandy baby?"

And John Riggins must answer in all candor: " Don't know. Haven't seen her lately." And he still hasn't heard from her, either, even after sending a dozen roses as an apology to her at her Supreme Court office.

The apology came after the last time — the only time — he saw her, almost seven years ago, in January 1985, when Riggins, then a star running back for the Washington Redskins and the hero of their 1983 Super Bowl victory, was seated across the table from Justice Sandra Day O'Connor and her husband, John, at the black-tie National Press Club dinner in Washington. Riggins, trying to make conversation while inebriated, called out: "C'mon, Sandy, baby. Loosen up. You're too tight."

Then he got up to talk to her husband, but never quite made it around the table. He collapsed and fell asleep under a chair, in his tuxedo and cowboy boots, pinning the wife of Senator John Glenn into her seat — "I must have been like an 18-wheeler lying there," he recalled. He stayed there, snoring, for about an hour, though the Justice was gone by the time he was awakened and escorted from the premises by the security guards. (He also sent a dozen roses to Mrs. Glenn and the three or four other women at the table that night.)

Riggins spoke about his life and times earlier this week in the quiet of a Manhattan restaurant. Upon arrival, the 6-feet-3-inch Riggins, following the maitre d'hôtel as he once followed blockers, easily made his way between tables, busboys and waiters as easily as he shed tacklers on the football field. He weighs 240 pounds, just five pounds more than in his playing days, and it appeared that all he needed was to remove his turquoise bolo tie and black corduroy sports jacket and don helmet and pads to take his place in the Redskins backfield for their game this afternoon against the Giants in Robert F. Kennedy Stadium in Washington.

"In those days," said Riggins, "I thought people in Washington didn't allow themselves to enjoy a party. They were stiff. That wasn't my idea of a real hoe-down good time. I liked to have people swinging from the chandeliers. I'd like to think I've grown up a little since then."

The speaker when Riggins was motivated to take his snooze under the table happened to be the Vice President of the United States, George Bush. "He wrote me afterward," said Riggins, "and said something like 'Well, John, we all have our bad days.'"

Riggins, now 42 years old and retired from football for six seasons, told this story with a bit of a sheepish grin on his face, a broad, intelligent face with eyes that look as though they still, on occasion, might covet a chandelier.

Much has happened for Riggins since his last game in

THE GRIDIRON GAME

pro football, in December 1985: a recent divorce, difficulties accepting separation from his four children, living for a reclusive year and a half in a trailer on the Potomac River and perhaps some problems with alcohol. He has begun a career in radio (he does commentary on football on a radio talk show in Washington). And now, he hopes, to begin one in acting, too. He plans to move back to New York from his home in northern Virginia. Meanwhile, he still keeps an eye on football.

He wondered about the motivation of the Redskins for the Giants game today, one that is meaningless in the standing. "I know I'd be bored to tears right now if I was on the team."

Somehow, one got the feeling that he would, as he usually did, find something to relieve the boredom. He has been called variously "independent," "boorish," "witty," and, to be sure, "bibulous."

One time he wore an Afro, later a Mohawk, and sometimes he shaved his head bald.

He held out for all of one season, 1980, because the contract the Redskins offered wasn't to his liking. "And something else. It was a kind of revenge against the owners. There's a seamy side to football. There's the thing about when you're hurt and they stick a needle in your arm and say, 'O.K., go back out there.' And there's the way they treat the players, like some of my friends, who were dropped when they weren't of any more use. I had just gotten fed up with some of that stuff."

Riggins was a country boy from Kansas, from the small town of Centralia (population: 500), but had learned that he didn't have to do things in a small-town way, or the way others wanted him to. And that if he could carry a football, eventually people would come around to him. And it happened. The season after Riggins sat out, the Redskins paid him close to what he asked for and he would repay them by becoming one of their finest runners. He led them to Super Bowl XVII in January 1983, in which he made a spectacular 43-yard run against Miami that broke open the game in the fourth quarter and helped the Redskins win, 27-17. He ran for a total of 126 yards, then a Super Bowl record.

"Not many athletes have a big game in the biggest game there is," said Riggins, "and it changed my life in a number of ways. One of them was that it made Washington kind of a small town for me, Centralia all over again. I'd walk down the street and people would be calling 'Riggo.' You have to remember, Washington only has two things that most of the people there care about, government and the Redskins. And a lot of the time they don't care for the government."

Sometimes, Riggins' way of relieving his boredom was not always in his best interest. Riggins, as he admits, likes to drink, although he says that he is not an alcoholic. He is able to stop for long periods of time and then return to moderate drinking. "I've heard that an alcoholic is someone whose life and work is affected by drinking," he said. "I don't think my work was. I mean, I played 14 years in the NFL, and I was the oldest running back, at 36, to gain more than 1000 yards. Me and the woolly mammoth."

He still holds records for most touchdowns scored in a season, 24, in 1982, and his 104 career rushing touchdowns are third behind Walter Payton's 110 and Jim Brown's 106.

He drank regularly after practice. "To celebrate," he said. "I was always looking for a reason to celebrate. And the Redskins understood that I did what they wanted me to do on the field, so they put up with my off-the-field stuff."

But his drinking did get him into a problem with the law. In one publicized case, in 1985, he was arrested as an intoxicated passenger in a car in Reston, Va. "At least I had the good sense not to drive in my condition," he said, "but the police stopped the car because they felt my friend was too drunk to be driving. And when they were going to arrest him, I said, 'Hoo, I'm not going to let him take the rap.' So I got into trouble, too."

He said he didn't think his problems with his divorce had anything to do with drinking. "My ex-wife may disagree with me," he said, "but I think she might disagree me on a lot of issues."

When they separated in January 1989, Riggins bought a 21-foot trailer and went to live on it on a piece of property that he owns along the Potomac River in Virginia. "When I moved out of the house, I couldn't see myself renting an apartment," he said. "I wanted to try living alone, isolated, like that." But he said he also lived in the trailer "for pecuniary reasons." "I had money from football," he said, "but I was never sure how far it would go."

He retired from football after the 1985 season and had not thought much of his future. He had a lot of time to think about this in his trailer, as he hauled water to drink. And he wondered about all this on freezing mornings in his sleeping bag when all the heat was off and the frost was on the window.

"And I thought, 'Well what do I do now?' The one thing I knew I didn't want to do was get out of that sleeping bag."

He seemed, to an outsider, the classic case of the man-child ex-athlete who can't grow up, and who was lost in the so-called real world. "I don't know about whether I had lost my way," said Riggins. "It was more like I never knew my way."

His whole life, he said, was playing football. "And playing football for as long as I did can give you a distorted view of life. I mean, I was fast and big and had good balance. I was a better animal than most. And I didn't even have to practice hard. But when you retire at 36, and everyone else is more or less just getting their legs in other endeavors, you wonder about yourself. I've often thought that a pro career should never go more than four years, like in college. Then you're forced to get on with your life in something else."

He had no real skills, other than being an entertainer. "That's what a football player is, isn't he?" asked Riggins.

In the summer of 1990, Riggins moved out of the trailer and into an apartment. He came up to New York, a place that had awed him and attracted him ever since he played for the Jets from 1971 to 1975. Riggins found a place to live in Chinatown and stayed there for about six months. He then moved back to Virginia. He was searching for something, and wasn't sure what.

He soon came to another realization. He wanted to be closer to his children. He sees them now once a week and sometimes on weekends.

Riggins has four children: two girls, ages 5 and 12, two boys, 17 and 8. The oldest, Bobby, is a high-school senior and a wide receiver on his high-school football team in Virginia.

"Now that I'm out of the game," said Riggins, "I realize more than ever how dangerous it is and how lucky I was to get out of it with relatively few injuries. I thought about this when Mike Utley of the Lions became paralyzed for life while blocking a few weeks ago. I'm not sure I want Bobby to play in college. But that's up to him."

Riggins has decided that he will try to be an actor. He has signed on with a theatrical agent, J. Michael Bloom of Manhattan, and plans to take acting lessons.

THE GRIDIRON GAME

Riggins said that he often thought that he played football to please his father, Gene Riggins, a depot agent, who was an avid sports fan.

"I know he dreamed of me or either of my two brothers becoming pro," said Riggins. His brothers, Frank and Billy, were, like John, running backs for the University of Kansas. "And I think I wanted to make my dad's dream come true. But acting I feel is for me, and me alone."

And if that doesn't work out? "Maybe I'll go back to Kansas and buy a farm, or a ranch. But I want to give this acting a real shot."

With dinner over, and most of the restaurant cleared of patrons, Riggins rose to leave. "You know," he said, "I wonder about Justice O'Connor sometimes. I did make a fool of myself that night, but I wonder if, on the flip side, she's a little more festive at a party. All I know is, she gave me a little smile when I suggested she loosen up. It was one of those Rodney Dangerfield looks that says, 'Cute kid. Now I know why tigers eat their young.'"

He laughed, and, in turquoise bolo tie and black jacket and black kangaroo cowboy boots, walked out into the cool New York night, the old football player, but still a young man, in search of a cab, and maybe of himself, too.

1991

Jim Brown with Hal Lebovitz
Ernie Davis

We were on our way back from Elmira, New York, in a four-engine plane chartered by the Cleveland Browns football team. We had flown there — our coaches, and the players who lived around Cleveland — to attend the funeral of a teammate who had never played a game with us.

Leukemia had taken Ernie Davis at the age of twenty-three.

At Elmira we had seen a city stop to pay him tribute. People had filled and surrounded the First Baptist Church, where funeral services were held; they had lined the road to Woodlawn Cemetery, where Ernie was buried. A complete silence had fallen over Elmira.

Except for the hum of the motors, our plane was equally quiet. It was a place and a time for contemplation. Ernie Davis in his 23 years captured the heart of his home town. In the few months he spent with us in Cleveland he made more friends than a man does in a lifetime.

His impact — an impact he didn't try to make — was so strong that Arthur Modell, owner of the Browns, broke down and cried at the news that Ernie was gone. Ernie's roommate, John Brown, a giant of a football player, wept quietly. I was stunned beyond belief.

I've always felt the words "great" and "courage" have been overused and abused. I have never been one to take them idly. I say with the utmost sincerity: Ernie Davis, to me, was the greatest, most courageous person I've ever met.

Though death is sad and often tragic — and these elements were present in Ernie's death — his is not a sad story. He made our lives better, brighter and fuller because we were privileged to know him.

Ernie would rebel at my effort to tell about him. He never wanted to be singled out. He never wanted to be different. He never sought praise or acclaim. He shunned interviews and adulation. Even during his illness, when he wrote a story in an effort to reject sympathy (it was titled *I'm Not Unlucky*), he worried afterward that readers might have misinterpreted it as bragging, or as an attempt to say he was something special.

But he was special. Samuel Clemens, better known as Mark Twain, is also buried in Woodlawn Cemetery, and he once said, "Among the three or four million cradles now rocking in the land are some which this nation would preserve for ages as sacred things, if we could know which ones they are."

Ernie's memory is being preserved. In Elmira the junior high school Ernie attended has been named after him. The All-America Football Game, held each summer in Buffalo (Ernie played in the first one 1962), has established a memorial trophy given in his name annually to "the player who most impressed his coaches with a general attitude of cooperation, leadership, cheerfulness and all-around conduct on and off the field." The idea for the award came from Buffalo citizens who had known Ernie personally and had found these qualities in him.

An Ernie Davis Leukemia Fund, affiliated with the American Cancer Society, has been created by the Cleveland Browns. The Browns started it with a large contribution, and it is the hope of Arthur Modell, who conceived it, and the American Cancer Society that "Ernie Davis Chairs" will be set up in several medical schools for research devoted to the cause and cure of leukemia.

Why is Ernie's memory being "preserved for the ages?" Because he died at the prime of his life of leukemia? Because he was a fine football player?

Not really. Countless others suffered equally from this blood disease. And in football he never did get to prove himself professionally, the goal Ernie had set for himself.

Obviously, his illness and his athletic achievements are emotionally involved in his memory. But it's so much more than that. It's the way in which he carried himself through his life. Always humble, but with dignity, pride and strength. And always with an unforgettable selflessness, a compassion for others.

I met him for the first time when I was a senior at Syracuse University. He was a high school star at Elmira, a scholastic All-America as a junior. It was suggested I visit Ernie and tell him about Syracuse.

I met him at the home of Anthony DeFilippo, an Elmira attorney and a Syracuse alumnus. Tony DeFilippo was like a father to Ernie (Ernie's father had died shortly after he was born). Somehow I had expected Ernie to be a smart, flashily dressed teenager. Instead I met a clean-cut young man, dressed in the manner of an Eastern college student.

Jim Brown with Hal Lebovitz

This might be a funny thing, but his neatness made an indelible impression on me.

He also seemed to be a shy individual. I found this to be not completely true. His shy manner was really a reticence toward acclaim. To friends he always opened up.

I talked to Ernie differently from the way coaches would. I told him exactly what he could expect at Syracuse, the good and the bad. We talked about the social life and how a Negro was treated. Ultimately he decided to attend Syracuse, mostly because of Tony DeFilippo's influence. The big thing that worried him about going there was me. I had broken football records there, become an All-America. My shadow fell on Ernie. Would he be better than Jim Brown? Did he want to be another Jim Brown? These were the questions immediately asked by the sportswriters.

By saying the wrong things, he could have put both of us in a funny spot. He handled the delicate situation perfectly. He simply said he respected my ability, but that he wanted to make it on his own, in his own way. To me, this is the mark of a great athlete and I developed the deepest respect for him.

I rarely saw him play at Syracuse, but I followed his accomplishments. He broke all my records, he was an All-America, he was the first Negro ever to win the Heisman Trophy, awarded annually to the outstanding college football player in the nation. He led the graduation parade at Syracuse, an honor given to the senior who contributes the most scholastically and athletically; he received and, of course, accepted an invitation to meet President Kennedy.

Though I rarely saw Ernie play football, I did meet him from time to time. He always talked to me about pro football and told me that more than anything else he wanted to play pro football.

THE GRIDIRON GAME

After his senior season, he was the No. 1 draft choice in the National Football League and the American Football League, and he also became the top target of the Canadian Football League. The Browns, in a trade with Washington, received the NFL rights to sign Ernie, and Modell signed him for a $15,000 bonus (he sent the check to his mother so she could pay off her obligations) plus a three-year contract calling for an additional $65,000. It was an excellent contract, but he turned down a better one from Buffalo. He could have forced Modell to go higher, but, truthfully, Ernie would have signed for less if necessary. He simply wanted to play for the Browns.

Probably no one was closer to Ernie than his roommate, John Brown. They were buddies at Syracuse before coming to Cleveland. (Ernie always ran the two names together and called him "Johnbrown.") John told me: "Some people play for money or for other reasons. Ernie wanted to play pro football just because he wanted to play. He loved it."

Ernie came to our early summer camp for advance schooling, then headed for Chicago where he was to play with the College All-Stars against the Green Bay Packers, the NFL champions. A few days before the game he developed symptoms that required an examination. The doctors at Evanston General Hospital diagnosed his illness immediately as leukemia, and called Modell, who went there with Tony DeFilippo.

Ernie wasn't told what he had. He thought it might be mumps or mononucleosis. But he knew he was out of the game and when Modell and DeFilippo came into his room they found him sitting at the edge of the bed, crying.

This was the only time he showed loss of composure. "They really were tears of disappointment," Modell told me later. "He was bewildered, confused. He felt fine and wanted to play but was told he couldn't. He was unable to understand why."

I knew almost immediately that Ernie had leukemia. Modell and the doctors leveled with his close friends and sportswriters, asking them for Ernie's sake to keep it off the record. Otherwise, he was certain, the news would leak out.

I can't say enough about the manner in which Modell treated Ernie. He had become fond of him during their period of negotiations and now regardless of the blow Ernie's loss was to the Browns, the team president wanted to do everything possible, at whatever the cost, to make Ernie's few remaining months (the prognosis given at Evanston) as pleasant as possible.

He had Ernie flown back to Cleveland for further examination and to put him in an environment among friends. We visited him in Marymount Hospital that night. John Brown and John Wooten and I drove in from training camp to sit in Ernie's room. We turned on the television set and watched the All-Stars play the Packers in the game Ernie had so wanted to participate in.

Not once did he talk about himself, or his disappointment. Instead he told us about players on the All-Star team, how big they were and their abilities. He was obviously touched when it was announced that the Packers had voted to award him the game ball.

Ernie was allowed to come to camp to visit us, but had to return to the hospital each evening. We often asked ourselves: "Does he know how sick he really is?"

The question was answered for us silently a few weeks later. He was sent to Bethesda, Maryland, for a checkup and when he returned, Modell and DeFillipo found on the back seat of the car, where Ernie had been sitting, a booklet of burial masses. It had slipped out of his pocket.

THE GRIDIRON GAME

In Cleveland, Dr. Victor Ippolito, the Browns' team physician, called in Dr. Austin Weisberger, a professor of medicine at Western Reserve University and one of the nation's foremost hematologists, to take over Ernie's case. As it was with everyone who got to know Ernie, a close friendship grew between the two.

We continued to see Ernie as often as possible. He no longer was confined to the hospital, going there only for medication and examinations. He moved into an apartment with John Brown and attended our exhibition games.

Suddenly, something happened that Dr. Weisberger still describes as "semi-miraculous." Ernie entered a state of complete remission, meaning tests showed his blood count normal in all respects. He explained it's not uncommon for adults to become remissive but the completeness of Ernie's, he said, was remarkable. How long the temporary state would last was a matter of speculation.

It was agreed by the doctors and Modell that it was time to tell Ernie exactly what he had. There was too much whispering. John Brown told us Ernie went to a movie and a stranger came up and asked him: "Are you Ernie Davis?"

According to John: "Ernie never wanted anybody to make a fuss over him so he said, 'No.'

"The man said, 'You're lucky, because Ernie Davis has leukemia and he's going to die in six months.'

"Ernie replied quietly: 'I'm Ernie Davis and I'm not going to die.'"

He explained to John afterward: "I didn't want to hurt that man but it might keep him from being cruel to somebody else."

Dr. Weisberger broke the news to Ernie gently. The doctor and Arthur Modell described the meeting to me. The doctor cushioned the blow by telling Ernie the remission was so complete he could now play football. This news brightened him considerably but it didn't eliminate the fact that he finally knew he had leukemia.

Ernie's first comment was: "Can I lick it"

Dr. Weisberger replied that people have been known to live normal lives for a long time with it.

Ernie perspired a little and remained quiet.

The doctor said, "You're an intelligent person. You must have had some inkling."

"Yes, I thought about the possibility," Ernie said. "But I made myself stop thinking about it. I had made up my mind that whatever I had I was going to have to live with it and make the most of it."

Dr. Weisberger told me: "I don't believe for a minute that he wasn't upset, but he never showed it. Not once."

Ernie asked that his illness be kept a secret but he was told his ability to play football would be a lift to other leukemia patients and he finally agreed to a carefully worded statement to be issued to reporters.

Ernie began to work out every day. He'd run and do calisthenics. He seemed in better shape than many of us. He ran longer and harder. We played golf together, went bowling. It was amazing to me that in a relatively short time he knew as much about the defenses of the other teams as I knew. He studied the game thoroughly. I'd say, "What do you think of so-and-so as a linebacker" and he'd give me a complete analysis which often helped me. He was absorbed in football.

But it soon became evident to all of us that, despite the doctor's full permission, Paul Brown wasn't going to give Ernie a chance to play. On the practice field Ernie would be forced to condition by himself. Paul didn't bring him into the huddles even as a listener. Undoubtedly he had his reasons.

At the end of the season Paul Brown was fired. A great majority of our players, myself included, said publicly we were glad of the change. We felt we couldn't play our best under him. But Ernie Davis, the man who suffered the most, the man who wanted to play pro football more deeply than any of us — if only for a token quarter to see his dream come true — said only: "From the little I know of Paul Brown, I think he is a fine gentleman."

These words from the man who always hopefully signed his autograph, "Ernie Davis, Cleveland Browns, 1962," were not said in cover-up. Ernie always said what he meant. Many times in private conversations I would try to probe him about Paul Brown. He always spoke respectfully about the coach.

When Paul Brown had made the trade for the draft rights for Ernie, he planned to use a "two-fullback" offense. The Packers had that offense with Jim Taylor and Paul Hornung. Ours was to be built around Jim Brown and Ernie Davis. I didn't agree with it completely. I wasn't for it or against it. I wanted to study Ernie on the football field — to analyze him, to see what he had — before I decided whether it would work. In football I never got the chance.

But on the basketball floor I found out this man would have been all he was cracked up to be. We have a Cleveland Browns basketball team which plays during the winter. Ernie had the doctor's okay to join us. In our first game we met a strong team, one that had beaten us the year before. The gym was packed. Ernie was like a tiger on the floor. He never let up. Near the end of the game I got a rebound and the instant he saw me grab it he was streaking for the other basket. He continued to play that way and we won the game by a couple of points.

The way he fought I knew I didn't have to look at him in

a football uniform to realize what might have been. I've thought about it often. He could have contributed so much.

I didn't get to play much basketball with him after that game. In February he began to slip out of his remissive state and was advised by the doctor to stop playing basketball "for a while." All Ernie said to Dr. Weisberger when he was told that further blood therapy would be required again — medication and transfusions — was "Darn."

"That was the only complaint, literally and truly, that Ernie ever made in all the times I saw him," the doctor told me. Not once was a tranquilizer needed. The doctor said Ernie's refusal to complain made it necessary to evaluate his condition by examination of the blood rather than symptoms which Ernie might relate. He always told the doctor, "I feel fine. I feel strong." He didn't want to be a bother to us.

That's how he was with us. We knew the remission had disappeared but he wouldn't let on. He continued to play golf with us, to go to movies and parties with us. He always was part of the crowd. Once he had a piece of cotton in his nose to stop some bleeding. He did it with his hand so we wouldn't see it.

When he needed transfusions, he wouldn't stay in the hospital overnight. He didn't want anyone to know about them. John Brown told me: "If I didn't know from the doctor that Ernie was sick I'd swear he was perfectly normal. He never gave any indication that anything was wrong." He wanted to preserve an image of strength. He didn't want anybody to see him lying down.

Ernie was religious and went to church regularly, and John says each night he would shut the door to his room for a few moments of privacy, probably for prayer.

Just once after the remission disappeared, Ernie hinted at his illness. He and "Johnbrown" were conversing in the quiet of their apartment. John told me: "I was talking about marriage, life, the hard road you have to travel, you're sometimes afraid to take a step."

Ernie said softly: "I may not make it, John. But that doesn't mean I have to quit trying."

This was his philosophy, the reaction of a fierce competitor. And he didn't quit. He refused to remain idle. He talked about next year when he would be playing for the Browns. He went to the Browns' office and offered to help in any manner he could. Modell assigned him to study movies of opposing teams, similar to the analysis done by the coaching staff. He was given the films of our games with the Giants and Redskins and he worked on them for two weeks at home and in the office.

The job he did caused Dick Evans, one of our coaches, to doubt the work had been done by someone without any coaching experience. "It was a helluva study," Dick told me. "He put down every move. It's really fantastic."

The staff considers it a major contribution for the 1963 season. If we are more successful against these two tough teams, Ernie will have played a vital part.

Two weeks before he died Ernie bought a set of golf clubs and displayed the set as a "bargain." He was becoming a good golfer. He took me to a clothing store in New York where we purchased car coats for the "coming winter." He talked about the new car he would buy "next year."

He also told Dr. Weisberger he planned to get married. He and a lovely Syracuse coed, Helen, were deeply in love. The doctor said it might be a good idea and mentioned he would like to talk to the girl. Ernie came back from the visit and reported he had decided to wait until next year. The doctor feels Ernie changed his mind because he didn't want to take the chance of being a burden on her. I believe this, too, for I know she would gladly have married Ernie had he asked.

Toward the end Ernie's neck swelled up and he was in great pain. But all he said was he might be having some tooth trouble.

Two days before he died he had an appointment with Dr. Weisberger. John Brown woke him up to remind him of the appointment, and then left for work. Before going to the doctor, Ernie went to the Stadium to visit Modell. "This was strange," Modell told me later. "He usually phoned first. Now I realize he was coming in to say 'good-bye.'"

When John Brown came home that night he found a note from Ernie: "Have to go to the hospital for a few days. Don't tell anybody. I'll see you around."

That was all. None of us ever saw Ernie alive again, and yet I find it difficult to realize he's gone. Maybe it's because I never saw him sick or never heard him complain. The way he acted he had me believing he'd make it. Even now I find myself talking about him in the present: "Ernie is," not "Ernie was."

He was the finest guy I've ever met. Not because he was always smiling, soft-spoken, gentle, seemingly shy. But because he was so honest, so realistic, so considerate of others. Simply by being himself he won over people who were hard, suspicious and critical. And he did it without trying. He wasn't a middle-of-the-roader, still he was like a connecting link between groups of guys.

With Ernie around there were no cliques.

I knew Ernie when he was perfectly healthy. I knew him when he was sick. I watched him when I knew he had leukemia but he didn't. I watched him after he found out. I tried to see a difference. There wasn't any. He asked for nothing, wanted no special consideration but always was grateful for whatever he received. And his greatness was that no one ever tried to take advantage of his good heart.

The dictionary defines courage as "a mental or moral strength enabling one to venture, persevere and withstand danger, fear or difficulty firmly or resolutely." Ernie's actions fit this definition. He took his illness on his own shoulders, carried it, lived normally, simply. It was a tremendous thing to watch.

People say, "Hate me or love me but don't be indifferent to me." Ernie asked for none of this. To go without complaining, without a fuss — this is the greatest courage.

When a person as fine as Ernie, who had so much to live for, is taken away at such an early age, the natural reaction of his friends is: "Why did it have to be him?" John Brown confessed he gave this question much thought and finally concluded:

"Everybody was born with a purpose. Perhaps his was to make an impact on the sports world, on all of us. We let little things bother us. Here Ernie had a real big thing — he was fighting for his life. Still he never whined, never felt sorry or himself. When I feel low I think of how Ernie stood up under his burden and it gives me strength. He's an inspiration to me. I'm a better man because I knew him."

Arthur Modell keeps a large photo of Ernie above his desk at the Browns' office. "When I need a little extra lift I think of him," he told me.

Ernie's life has been an inspiration to me, too, but not in the same way as it has inspired John. I'm at a stage of life where I think I know myself pretty well. I know I'm not as high class as Ernie. I'm basically a skeptical person. I've seen so much hypocrisy, so many phonies, so many pseudo guys. Then I see this Ernie Davis, so straight, so honest, so genuinely considerate. I've looked deep into this guy and what's there is real. And this is where he's been an inspiration to me.

I say to myself, "If there's one guy like that, there must be others. Maybe there are millions like him." Which is good. If so, this isn't such a bad world after all. There's a hope for it."

Maybe I'm not a better man, as such, for having known Ernie but at least now I have more faith in people. I've never been quite as honest as this guy. By his example, he taught me a greater tolerance and understanding of others.

Dr. Weisberger told me he recently received a letter from a little boy which touched him deeply. It read, "I met Ernie Davis. He was so nice. I loved him. Here is twenty-five cents in his name to fight leukemia. I'll never forget him."

Neither will I.

1963

Chris Cobbs

Winslow Hits Wall and Keeps Going

Kellen Winslow felt worse pain when he suffered a broken leg. And he felt more fatigue when he worked a 16-hours shift as a laborer in a bullet-making factory.

But never had he felt so near death as he did during and after the Chargers' 41-38 win over Miami Saturday night.

With one of the truly Herculean efforts in pro football history, Winslow caught 13 passes for 166 yards and one touchdown and deflected a field goal on the last play of the fourth quarter, thus sending the game into overtime. He did all this despite a medical chart that included a busted lip, a bruised shoulder, a pinched nerve, and a case of heat exhaustion and cramps that left him barely able to move.

And he managed to get off about as good a quip as humanly possible under the circumstances. "You mean I took that whuppin' for just 166 yards," he said in a voice that carried the mock-incredulity that became Muhammad Ali's signature inflection.

Winslow, in fact, said he was reminded of Ali's fight against Joe Frazier, the Thriller in Manilla. Afterward, Ali had said he never felt so near death, and Winslow said that was true of his condition, too.

"I feel like I've been to the mountain top," Winslow said, "but gracious, I'm not sure I looked over it."

"It was a matter of who had the most will to win, and I would have kept pushing myself until we did.

"We had a chapel service this morning, and I remember the man saying we should play in the name of the Lord, for His glory, and push ourselves until we couldn't push anymore."

On a more secular level, Winslow said he was driven by the taunts and gestures of Dolphin fans and players. "It was just ridiculous, they were worse than the Oakland fans," he said.

Asked if a game such as this could make the Chargers a team of destiny, he replied, "I have felt all along we were that kind. We just took a different route."

Winslow received treatment for his assorted ailments before doing a live TV interview in the locker room. After the bright TV lights were extinguished, he turned and leaned against the wall, and seemed near fainting before he was helped away from another 15 minutes of therapy.

When he returned to his dressing stall to chat with reporters, he said he could barely talk because he had to have his lip sewed up, and it was still numb from the anesthetic.

Still, he answered questions patiently for 10-15 minutes, despite the pain that wracked his entire body.

1982

Chris Dufresne
❧
Young Blood

On Sunday, Sept. 29, 1991, shortly after 4 p.m., quarterback Steve Young of the San Francisco 49ers disappeared into a dark tunnel — man, was it ever — leading to locker rooms of the Los Angeles Memorial Coliseum. His cleats clacked on the concrete, a lonely walk illuminated only by the soft afternoon light on the playing field outside. He'd been chased into the catacomb by the long shadow of Joe Montana.

He had waited for what seemed an eternity for his chance and, now, what a mess he'd made. Young had worn a Chisholm-sized trail pacing the sidelines behind Montana since 1987, the year the quarterback-in-waiting arrived in San Francisco, ostensibly to rescue the franchise. Forty-Niners Coach Bill Walsh, the bon vivant, had tastefully handpicked Young as successor to Joe, whose brilliant career appeared doomed after back surgery in 1986.

Young's presence, however, had a faith-healer's effect on Montana, who rose from the trainer's table more than once to add two more Super Bowl titles to the pair he'd already delivered to San Francisco's rapturous fans. With those dagger-blue eyes, Montana kept Young in his competitive cross hairs for four more seasons. Gray flecks crept into the understudy's mop-top before a tendon tear in Montana's throwing elbow finally opened a crack in the huddle in 1991.

But come the late September game in Los Angeles that year, the legend-replacement business was going belly up. The 49ers were 2-2 entering the Raiders game, and fair-weathered San Francisco fans were almost afraid to come outside. Young responded with an odorous performance, a 12-6 loss in which he forced passes Montana would never have considered. In a last chance for redemption, a Montana-esque drive to victory, Young pushed his team to the Raider 19-yard line but left it stranded with 1:48 to play when a fourth-down pass fell incomplete.

No one had to remind Steve what Joe would have done. But someone did.

In the 49ers locker room, at the end of the dark corridor, defensive end Charles Haley flew into rage. He screamed at Young, cursed him, was so upset that he put his fist through a wall. Finally, exhausted, Haley broke down and wept, then curled into a fetal position on the floor, refusing to move. Ronnie Lott, the former 49er safety who had recently signed with the Raiders, had to be summoned from the L.A. locker room to console his onetime teammate.

"I just saw Charles go off," Young remembers of the incident. "I didn't know it was pointed at me at all. I was there. I didn't know he was picking me out. People said that later. I saw it. He just lost it. He was just really frustrated I guess."

You thought replacing Joe Montana was going to be easy?

Haley, with his unique body language, was saying it couldn't be done.

"It was hard," Young says of that day, "but I continually reminded myself, 'Welcome to what it takes.' I didn't want to walk away from it. I could have, but I didn't want to."

Young swears the darkest days are over now. Montana has gone to Kansas City, and Young is now the undisputed leader of the 49ers. He has emerged from the tunnel. No one of late has curled himself into a fetal position. In the Bay Area, this is progress.

⁂

The scoundrel is a brilliant athlete, educated and religious, a law student and voracious reader. He doesn't smoke or drink. He's so clean he squeaks. Friends call him the Eighth Wonder of the World because he might be the only known 31-year-old single Mormon.

He has no warrants outstanding, a generous heart and a warm smile. He is a millionaire 20 times over but has never owned a new car or a decent haircut. He gives freely his time and money, comforts old women in wheelchairs and huddles with Navajos who live in mud huts on Utah reservations.

They'd name streets after him some places. But in San Francisco, Steve Young to many is Public Enemy No. 1.

His crime? Replacing Joe Montana.

Happens to everyone. Seasons change. Quarterbacks get old. Unfortunately, legends do not. From George Washington to John Wooden, we know that replacing a legend in America folklore can sometimes be more difficult than becoming one. We are, by nature, myth makers.

"People here thought Joe would play until he was 70

years old," says Art Spander, longtime sports columnist for the *San Francisco Examiner*. "In a way, Steve Young became the Antichrist."

Montana ruled the kingdom of the 1980s. He transformed a perennial loser into a four-time Super Bowl champion with his flair for the dramatic and a ballet dancer's grace at the quarterback position. In a game of 300-pound brutes, Montana was poetry, almost effete — his style a perfect pairing for erudite San Franciscans who broke bread and sipped Chardonnay at Candlestick Park as their maestro conducted.

Forty-Niner games were concertos, with Montana lofting rainbow passes, perfectly arced and timed so that a receiver could catch a ball without having to break stride. Montana was grace, cool under pressure, a poker face who could tear an opposing team's heart out without changing expression.

Off the field, he was a relative wallflower — media-shy, reticent, never giving away too much. No one can ever recall Montana uttering a memorable line. Like Garbo's, his silence fueled the mystique. Joe let his Super Bowl rings do the talking.

By contrast, Young is a bull in Montana's china shop, a throwback to the old NFL leatherheads. He comes fully equipped with thick legs, wide-receiver speed, a quick wit and an inquisitive mind. Heck, Young even likes sportswriters. Compared to Montana, Young was a fork in an electrical socket. While Montana soothed 49ers fans with his style, Young makes them sweat with his antics. This has become unsettling to the local wine sippers.

Actually, it is not Joe but Steve, a soon-to-be lawyer and book lover, who seems more culturally suited to San Francisco. You picture Young-the-scholar bundled in a cardigan on a chilly summer day, sipping decaffeinated at the local coffee house, paging through the autobiography of Malcom X.

Young has fallen madly for San Francisco. Unfortunately, the city had already fallen for another. And no sweet-talkin', charity-givin', clean-livin' Morman was going to change that overnight, whatever his stats.

Young has made his mark as one of the game's grittiest and greatest running quarterbacks. In 1988, a breathtaking (Young's breath) 49-yard touchdown run against the Minnesota Vikings was judged by NFL Flims as the best run of the last 25 years. But it was only through diligence that Young became a polished passer. Putting both quarterback skills together has made him the most feared offensive player in today's game, a fact that ultimately made even Joe Montana expendable.

Sid Gillman, the Hall of Fame coach and quarterback guru, says Young is perhaps the best running passer ever, joining an elite trio with former Minnesota Viking great Fran Tarkenton and the Philadelphia Eagles' Randall Cunningham. "I don't think anybody's able to run the way he runs," says Gillman, who was Young's coach in 1984 with the Los Angeles Express of the now-defunct United States Football League.

Bill Walsh reinvented the passing game, using short, precisely timed patterns to control the field and the clock, and George Seifert, his successor, adopted that system when Walsh left the pro game to coach at Stanford. Young "fits into that plan beautifully," Gillman points out.

Young's passes would never spiral like Montana's had, but no quarterback could match Young's gifts as a runner. His legs were his trump card, and he needed it. Young has since refined his style, hanging longer in his pocket of blockers, looking for his receivers. The result: Last year, he rushed for 537 yards and passed for 3,465. His quarterback efficiency rating ranked fifth-best in league history.

Winning over his 49er teammates was another matter. Jerry Rice, the NFL's premier pass-catcher and Montana's favorite target, admitted that he had difficulty adjusting to passes that were not as precise as Joe's. But Young and his teammates sorted out their problems during last season, which took them as far as the National Football Conference championship.

Except one. The Super Bowl problem.

"Anywhere else, Steve Young is a hero," the 49ers' veteran lineman Jesse Sapolu said after the NFC title game loss to Dallas last January. "But he plays here in the footsteps of No. 16, so anything less than a Super Bowl win is not going to be enough for anybody. It's not fair. But I guess that's life."

San Francisco is in denial.

૨&

Young plops his dinner tray down on a mess hall table in the community college cafeteria, takes a curious whiff at what he guesses is cod, then digs into another plate of questions. A midday workout has given him a case of the slows. Air conditioning has forced him into a two-piece sweat suit, the collar upturned to keep the chill off his neck. Outside, a hot August afternoon has cooled into evening. Practice is over, the day soon to follow, yet you wonder if the sun ever really sets on the 49er quarterback who replaced Joe.

"You get used to the pace," Young explains in an interview here at the team's training camp in Rocklin, outside Sacramento, before the 1993 season began last month. "It wasn't easy. None of it was easy. I don't want to make it sound like I'm oblivious to everything. I'm not. But something makes me turn back into the fire and say: 'I'm going back in again. It's hot, but I'm going back in.' I don't know. Maybe I don't know any better."

Montana the 49er is gone, having requested and received a trade to the Kansas City Chiefs last April when it became clear that he would not be the No. 1 quarterback for San Francisco. To get him, Kansas City gave up a first-round draft choice for 1993, a third-round draft choice in 1994 and safety David Whittmore.

But even with their hero gone, Montana zealots swamp sports-talk radio and fire off letters to San Francisco editors. Lowell Cohn, A *Chronicle* columnist, recently received this indictment from a fan:...and don't fool yourselves into thinking just because Steve is the starting QB us Montana supporters will rush to his side saying, 'We're not worthy,' because you would be deadly wrong. Many of us just don't like Steve Young and never will because he is a kiss-ass."

The evidence against Young is flimsy at best: In two seasons as starter in place of Montana — who, remember, was unable to play because of injuries — Young became the first quarterback ever to lead the NFL in passing in consecutive seasons. In the second, 1992, he threw 25 touchdown passes and seven interceptions (Montana, in his best season as 49ers starter, never threw fewer than eight interceptions). Young was named the league's Most Valuable Player, leading his team to a 14-2 regular season record.

Yet, as the 49ers rolled toward the playoffs, talk had returned to Montana, then 36, out with injuries for nearly two seasons but itching to make another comeback. In the team's final regular season game against Detroit at Candlestick Park, Montana trotted on the field to a hero's welcome and threw two touchdown passes in the second half.

Young played nervously in a first-round playoff victory over the Washington Redskins. He says Montana's presence had nothing to do with his jitters: "It really didn't." You wanted to believe him.

In the conference title game against Dallas, Young played well enough to win, passing for 313 yards. But the Cowboys prevailed, 30-20, over a collapsing 49er defense, and the wolves sniffed for a scapegoat. "He didn't win the Super Bowl," columnist Spander explains. "It is his fault because Joe 'would have.' This guy (Young) is good. But it's like replacing Vince Lombardi. It's like replacing John Wooden. You all know that story — you can't do it."

After the Dallas loss, a disconsolate Young walked down another dark hallway, the recurring metaphor of his career, this one leading to the players' parking lot at Candlestick. Outside, he posed for a photo, kissed a woman in a wheelchair. Columnist Cohn followed the quarterback and heard a member of the stadium cleanup crew tell him: "One day you can fill Joe's shoes."

A few months later, the old magician decided to shop his wares around the league, and 49ers owner Edward DeBartolo Jr. did not stand in his way. Montana, after talking with a handful of clubs, settled on the Chiefs. Then, at the last minute, the 49ers got misty-eyed and offered Montana his job back — No. 1 quarterback. The proclamation was unfurled April 18 to a blare of media trumpets. Seifert named Montana the "designated starter," a decree that effectively sent the NFL's MVP back to the bench.

While the city was gripped with Montana fever for 48 hours, Young was in Provo, cramming for a law school final at BYU. "Everyone was asking, 'What were you thinking?'"

Young remembers. "Well, I kind of missed it. Which probably was good. It was a very bizarre time."

It ended when Joe, perhaps skeptical of the 49ers' 11th-hour promise, decided to stick with the Chiefs. (DeBartolo has since vowed that Montana will return at the end of his career to be honorably retired in a 49er uniform.)

Young, when it was over, dipped into his seemingly endless supply of positive thoughts, insisting that he never felt betrayed by the 49er management. After all, he reckoned, the club signed him to the richest contract in football last July, a five-year deal worth $26.5 million. OK, so Montana never cozied up to him through the years. OK, so Joe once told a reporter that Young was "on a big push for himself." Young rolls with the punches. He says he and Montana never exchanged a cross word. And what of Montana's cold shoulder? "I can't stop it. We're two hyper-competitive people....I don't feel any anger. I just don't. The impact he's made on my football career is pretty great. I recognize that and move on. I think it will be fine. I really do."

With no intention of changing football history, Ted Tollner went for a jog one afternoon in January, 1980. He was the new quarterback coach at Brigham Young, and as he was turning laps on the indoor track in the field house, he came upon a group of hopeful BYU quarterbacks tossing footballs in an unsupervised workout. Tollner was window shopping, or evaluating, not truly tampering, which might have drawn the wrath of the NCAA.

"I'm not going to say I didn't stop once in a while," says Tollner, the former USC coach and a current Rams assistant. The kid who caught his eye was a raw left-hander who was making no progress and thinking of quitting the program in disgust and going off on a two-year Mormon mission.

The young lefty, Steve Young, a scrub-faced freshman, was listed as the eighth-string quarterback behind starter Jim McMahon. LaVell Edwards, the BYU coach, was preparing to switch Young to defensive safety. Steve was practicing both positions during this winter of his discontent.

Then Tollner jogged by, fortuitously while the freshman was taking an offensive turn. He was intrigued with Young's athleticism and quick release. "I either like a guy or not," Tollner says, "but I was pretty strong with my opinion of him." He talked Edwards out of moving Young to defense. And Young never went on his Mormon mission. Still hasn't.

Everyone assumed that the quarterback's road was paved with Mormon influence. He was, most folks at BYU knew, the great-great-great grandson of the church leader for whom the school was named. More than once, he's heard: "He's related to Brigham Young." More than once, people have whispered that he had "a free ticket."

"Probably everyone has a story like this," he suggests, "but I easily could have quit and no one would have blinked."

Why didn't he? "My dad wouldn't let me." Nor would Tollner.

Young, a tremendous athlete, had only one flaw as a quarterback: He didn't know how to throw. He had been a running quarterback at high school in Connecticut. But he was a quick study and soon learned to pass by mimicking McMahon, himself now an NFL veteran. By his senior season, Young had developed into the nation's top college quarterback and finished second in voting for the Heisman Trophy. It was a long, strange trip.

Jon Steven Young was born in Salt Lake City, his family

moving to Greenwich, Conn., when Steve was 8. He is oldest of five children. His father, LeGrande, is a corporate lawyer.

The relationship to Brigham Young was not a regular dinner-table topic, although Steve would later take it upon himself to read up on the subject. "He was the first one to learn how to settle a desert," Young says proudly. "Think about the deserts of the Southwest now. There were a lot of things he was kind of ingenious about. The stories of getting across the plains. The stories were brutal. He was a great leader, I think."

As leader of a religion in which the taking of multiple wives was once accepted practice, Brigham Young might be surprised to know that a distant descendant, a guy named Steve, will still be unmarried when he turns 32 this month.

"I should have got married in college," Young says, "it would have solved a lot of problems." He came within days of the altar in 1987 before slamming the brakes. "That's why you get engaged," he says, "to figure out if that's what you really want to do. It was a crash-and-burn deal. It wasn't pretty."

Young is saddled with the burden of being perhaps the nation's most visible Mormon. "I don't want to put that pressure on me, because religion is very personal," Young says. "But I think I'm one of the people that people look to."

He lives accordingly. Five years ago, he estimates, he was making 100 speeches a year to various youth groups. With more demands on his time now, he has reduced the number to about 20. As part of the contract he signed with the 49ers in July, Young will donate $1 million to a children's foundation he created in the Bay Area. Young says he has no choice in the matter: He is a role model.

Yet, unlike some religious athletes who lace their post-game quotes with biblical phrases, invoking God's will in victory or defeat, Young believes in the separation of church and sport. "I just feel that it should be more subtle. It's about being a good human being. It's almost too important to trivialize with football."

As a kid, he longed to earn the respect of the older kids on the block. His father, he says, never pushed him into sports and didn't care what his children did so long as they gave their best.

Having grown up poor, LeGrande taught his children the value of a dollar, a lesson that has served well his oldest son, the football star, who still lives a rather Spartan life for someone who's earned more than $25 million since turning pro.

Steve, the spendthrift, a snapshot: After years of renting a room from a teammate with the 49ers, Young finally purchased a home in Pal Alto last winter. Twenty-five hundred square feet. That's closet space at Aaron Spelling's.

Young entered professional football in 1984, during the midst of a bidding war between the NFL and the USFL, a spring league that sprouted in 1983. The L.A. Express not only offered Young the richest contract in football history to that point — a deferred deal worth $37.2 million through the year 2027, but also the chance to play immediately.

The Express was an off-field experience he'd like to forget. It began when he almost came to blows during negotiations with William Oldenburg, the team's bombastic owner. Young was so distraught after the ordeal that he contemplated not reporting. His father, the lawyer, stepped in. A deal is a deal, he said. So Young went along for a wild ride with the L.A. club.

Within a year, Oldenburg had run into financial difficulties and stopped paying his players. Until a new buyer could be found, the league's remaining owners took control of the franchise and agreed to pay salaries, but not other operational expenses. Water was shut off at the team's headquarters in Manhattan Beach for lack of payment. Weeds grew on the practice field for want of a groundskeeper. En route to a game at Pierce College, where the team was to be showcased for potential buyers in the San Fernando Valley, the bus driver pulled over and refused to proceed until he was paid up front, in cash. Young passed the hat around among his fellow millionaires and satisfied the demand.

The USFL folded after the 1986 season. But Young had been drafted before the 1985 season by the NFL's Tampa Bay Buccaneers, for whom he played in 1985 and 1986. The Buccaneers were the lowest of the lowly, an organization that lost a record 26 consecutive games in the 1970s. For two seasons, Young ran for his life on teams that went 4-28. He saw his 1987 trade to the 49ers as a career saver. He would learn to play quarterback from one of the game's great teachers, Walsh, and tutor behind the game's greatest quarterback, Montana.

That he would grow impatient as Montana refused to wilt would be a small price to pay. That following his ascension to the No. 1 spot he would be dissected under lights like a laboratory rat — well, it still beat digging ditches. That he would be judged in San Francisco not by league MVP awards but by Super Bowl titles was an acceptable term.

"That's the reason I'm here," Young says at the Rocklin practice field as he looks forward to the current season. "I've said that all along. Because that's what it's about. Don't walk away from it because the expectations are high."

Even during the worst of it, in 1991, as Young's agent was pleading for him to get out of San Francisco, Young refused to leave.

"I mean, the 49ers dogged me in April" with the offer to bring back Montana as No. 1, he says. "But think back to all the disasters that happened in the USFL and all the crazy weird situations that I've been in," Young says, trying to add some perspective. "This is like living in a huge mansion, and you see a mouse running by. It's no big deal. You know what I mean? The complaints here, by comparison, are not that huge."

₴

At the team's summer training camp at Sierra College in Rocklin, the faithful clung to chain-link fences separating them from their 49er heroes. Except something was missing. Someone.

Joe.

Nilo Velazquez, manager of the Sierra College Bookstore, guessed that training-season attendance at the camp had been halved, from about 80,000 to 40,000, because of Montana's absence. The fans who came shopped as though Montana had never left. They stood in long lines to get a crack at the team's souvenir shop, a double-wide mobile home behind the bleachers on the main field, where they gobbled up Montana-as-49er memorabilia: posters, $135 figurines, $32 silver medallions, key chains, license-plate holders, cigarette lighters, cups, plaques, wristbands.

Rick Oltmann, a Citrus Heights hydrologist and a 49er fan since 1956, was typical of the tortured, sporting a fire-engine red Kansas City Chiefs T-shirt and a gray 49ers baseball cap with red and gold trim. Oltmann said his children bought him the T-shirt so he could wear it in tribute to Montana. "He's one of a kind," Oltmann explains. "You can't expect people to live up to that level. Young could be the best quarterback the next five years, but he still won't be Joe."

Bill Bedwell, another sentimentalist, says the team should have kept the older Montana and traded Young. "I'm still pissed off," he says of the trade. "What has Steve Young proven to the city? Is he a winner?" Nothing personal. "He's real warm, not a show boater," Bedwell continues. "He's a mellow man, a gentle man, a confident man. But he A-I-N-'T Joe."

The passion for Montana goes beyond numbers. Fireman Joe rescued the 49ers from a football inferno. The Niners were the Bay Area's first professional franchise, born in 1946 as members of the All America Football Conference. The baseball Giants didn't arrive until 1958, the Oakland Athletics and once-Oakland Raiders not until the 1960s.

Spander of the *Examiner*: "Here's this town, this narcissistic town, thinks it's the greatest, Queen of the West, we have the best restaurants, we're elegant; L.A.'s a bunch of boors, Johnny-come-latelies...Meanwhile the team stinks. People go to the games basically to get drunk."

Walsh and Montana ushered in an era of elegance. Fans still drank, but now they ordered from a wine list. Coach and player came to the 49ers in 1979 at rock bottom. Walsh's first team went 2-14. His second improved to 6-10. But the following season, 1981, Walsh and Montana led the 49ers to the first of their four Super Bowl wins, the others following the 1984, 1988 and 1989 seasons. Montana's legend was born in the NFC title game in 1981, at Candlestick against Dallas, when he lofted a last-minute, game-winning, end-zone touchdown pass to Dwight Clark that would forever be known simply as "The Catch."

No one remembers that Montana threw three interceptions in the game.

"Joe Montana never threw an interception," says Ralph Barbieri, host of a lively weeknight sports talk show on KNBR radio. "Joe Montana never threw an incompletion. Nobody remembers any of this."

"It was like Joe invented football," Spander says. "Like someone once wrote years ago, Arnold Palmer invented golf. Nobody knew it existed. Joe personified, incarnate, was the 49ers."

The Montana myth swelled with each comeback, on and off the field. He returned miraculously from 1986 back surgery. In 1988, when he was hobbled again, Walsh seemed eager to plug Young into his sophisticated pass offense, as though to prove it was the system more than the man. But Young wasn't ready.

And when the team was sputtering with a 6-5 record, Montana returned again and the 49ers did not lose another game en route to their third Super Bowl, in which the quarterback led his team on a dramatic last-minute drive to victory.

The 49ers won the Super Bowl again the next season. Even though Montana missed almost two complete seasons in 1991 and 1992, 49er fans waited dutifully for his return.

"I liken it to those old Civil War stories," Spander says, "where they're waiting for their guys to come back, and the South will rise again. They kept waiting for Joe, and the Joe thing just swallowed them up, and two years ago it distracted this team something awful...."

How could Young forget Los Angeles? The Raiders. The

THE GRIDIRON GAME

Coliseum. Charles Haley.

Despite a 10-6 record, the 49ers didn't make the playoffs in 1991, grounds for quarterback deportation. Young might have thought his MVP performance last season would have eased the transition. The truth is: Any quarterback after Joe will be a Joe Schmo.

Even Most Valuable Players. Young could go on to win a Super Bowl and a Nobel Prize. Won't matter. Cripes, imagine the public outcry had Montana's replacement not been as great as Steve Young.

The 49ers will be Super Bowl contenders again this season. In San Francisco, it's the law. While the defense is suspect, the offense has shown no appreciable drop-off. In Dallas, the defending Super Bowl champion Cowboys appear vulnerable.

The patience of 49er fans will likely extend through the regular season, which the team started with two wins and a loss. But at playoff time, Montana time, expectations will soar. Comparisons will be inevitable.

It comes with the territory, this expanse of Montana.

"It kind of frustrates me," Young says, "because it's almost like a self-fulfilling prophecy. People keep asking: 'How does it feel not to get the respect? How does it feel?' and I go: 'I walk down the streets of San Francisco, and people are great.' They love the 49ers. They love what we're doing. They sense the same thing, that we're building on. Let's go. I get all of that, even more so every day. The toughest times are behind."

1993

Tom Junod
Montana Fading Out

I heard that Joe Montana was traveling to Brunei at the behest of the royal family, and I had an awful dream. I dreamed that Joe stood alone on desert sands in his helmet and shoulder pads and jersey, surrounded, at great distance, by oil barons in their Mercedeses and Rolls-Royces. And one by one, the barons got out of their cars, trudged up to Joe and demanded "Do me like you did Dwight Clark." And Joe couldn't say no, because the barons were paying extravagantly for his time, and so again and again, until day passed into night and the only lights were the headlamps of luxury automobiles, Joe was compelled to roll right, the way he did in his first NFC championship against the Dallas Cowboys, and lob a high lumpy spiral to leaping oilmen....who, encumbered by their robes and lack of experience, dropped every pass and became humiliated and wound up abandoning Joe to the winds that scour the desert clean at night.

Never mind that I had no idea where the hell Brunei

was and that the next morning, when I looked at a map, I saw that it's in the South Pacific, on the island of Borneo, and what I dreamed was desert is in fact occupied by rain forest. The dream spooked me. It carried the weight of omen, and when I finally met Joe, I asked him what he'd done there. He had gone with Herschel Walker, he said. He had stayed at the sultan's palace. He had played a lot of golf and had made a lot of money. He had been paid to throw the football to the sultan's nephew and to teach the nephew's children how to play the American game. The nephew had purchased equipment for the occasion, and he wanted Joe to suit up. *Suit up?* Well, sure — Joe was a football player, and so here, in the oil-rich Islamic sultanate of Brunei, Abode of Peace...here, across oceans, time zones, languages, religions, cultures....what was waiting for him was shoulder pads and gleaming black helmets...football stuff. C'mon, Joe — suit up! But Joe told the sultan's nephew that by the terms of his contract with the Kansas City Chiefs he was forbidden to wear the uniform of another team, any other team — it was a fib, but it worked — and so Joe and Herschel played in shorts and T-shirts while members of Brunei's royal family, augmented by the strongmen of the state security force, ran around in the brand-new helmets and shoulder pads.

I was frightened by the force of premonition. Yes, I know I should have been pleased for Joe; after all, not everyone can make a killing teaching monarchs how to throw a spiral. Still, the idea of Joe, Joe *Montana*, in the role of lucrative servitude...especially after that dream — well, it was unseemly. It was grotesque. It was the Mick drying out at Betty Ford, Ted Williams hawking his wares on QVC, Joe Willie hoofing in a dinner theater, Joe Louis squeezing hands at Caesars, Joe DiMaggio shilling for Mr. Coffee. As a young man, I could never watch a Mr. Coffee commercial without feeling a pang of misery; I had never seen the Yankee Clipper play, but I imagined that he must have been great *then*, because he sure wasn't great *now* — he looked bereft, like a defrocked priest: Joyless Joe DiMaggio. I did not feel sorry for him, however, as much as I felt for those who had loved him, who had adored him and had believed that his ineffable and defining greatness would somehow last forever.

Now it was time to feel sorry, in a strange way, for myself. You see, I'd had another dream about Joe — *our* Joe, *my* Joe — and his journey to Brunei, and this was the dream I had invested with my own hope and belief. I had dreamed that Joe had gone to Brunei on a mission of dire importance; that the sultan had summoned him personally, not for instruction or diversion but rather for survival, to quell an insurrection of infidels. I dreamed that he did not fail, because Joe, well, he *never* fails; that what Joe did on the football field, he would keep on doing, outside of football, outside of sport, forever; that he would just keep *playing*, in ever greater and more important arenas...diplomacy, espionage, politics, art, literature, music, whatever...and ride the whole supercool super-clutch mystic mojo of his own greatness — which, after all, is partially *our* greatness — into history....

I felt sorry for myself, of course, because once I'd met Joe Montana I realized that, as the cost and condition of his greatness, he had purged his brain of grandiose and debilitating dreams and that the only dreams he had left were dreams of refuge — from history, yes, and also from us.

※

To explain what I mean about the costs and conditions of Joe's greatness, I would like to tell two stories about him, both of which happen to concern Tim Barnett's ears. The first is about what makes Joe legendary and the second is about what makes him — efficiently, impressively, triumphantly, magically — limited. That both stories have an aural leitmotiv just goes to show how, in Joe's case, what is legendary and what is limited are intertwined and, in the end, indistinguishable.

Tim Barnett is a wide receiver for the Kansas City Chiefs. He has unusual ears. While unremarkable in size, they are whorled and flared, distinctly shell-like, and they are joined to his head at an angle that makes them look like afterthoughts. Once Joe became a Chief, he made it immediately clear that they amused him. He called Barnett "the Doberman," and Barnett, in truth, found some comfort in Joe's mockery. Joe had joined the Chiefs from the San Francisco 49ers, where he had won four Super Bowls and had worked with the finest cadre of pass-catchers in football, and Barnett was frankly afraid that Joe would turn up his nose at what the Chiefs offered in the way of wideouts. Now, here was Joe Montana, who was the greatest quarterback ever, calling Tim Barnett "the Doberman," and here was Tim Barnett — who was, well, Tim Barnett — calling Joe "Pinocchio," on account of his prodigious beak. On his very first day in Kansas City, Joe Montana had, in Barnett's mind, became a full-fledged member of the Chiefs.

❧

The first of our Joe Montana stories takes Tim Barnett's ears to San Diego, where, toward the end of last season, the Chiefs were playing the Chargers in a game crucial to Kansas City's playoff hopes. The Chiefs were behind by a field goal late in the game and had to score a touchdown to win.

THE GRIDIRON GAME

Now, as everyone, including Tim Barnett, knows, dire situations are Joe Montana's métier, and adversity is to Joe what spinach is to Popeye; still, a touchdown is a touchdown, and as Barnett says, "when you're behind, it distracts you." It is rather like a twelfth man has sneaked into the huddle, a gloomy, twitchy, pessimistic character who, as the quarterback calls the play, shakes his head and frowns and says, "That'll never work." Well, in San Diego on that day, the twelfth man had taken his place in the huddle and the Chiefs were looking at him and he was making faces and Joe...well, it was like Joe didn't see him, or if he did see him, he didn't let on. The San Diego crowd was whooping it up, flexing its din muscles, and Joe said to his teammates, "Don't worry about the clock, don't listen to the crowd, and let's have some fun." Then he looked at Barnett and said, "Sorry, Tim — I guess with those ears you *have to* listen to the crowd. I guess with those ears you can hear the *press box*. What are they saying up there?" The twelfth man, of course, was not amused; he slunk out of the huddle, took his seat on the bench and watched the Chiefs win the game.

The second Joe story takes place in a middle school in Kansas City, where Barnett's ears, in theory, should have had little relevance. Joe was there — along with Barnett and backup quarterback Steve Bono, Matt Blundin and Alex Van Pelt — as a favor to the Chiefs' offensive coordinator, Paul Hackett, or, rather, to Hackett's son Nate, a seventh grader. As part of a fund-raiser, Nate had auctioned off an opportunity to eat lunch with Joe Montana and the Chiefs. The five kids who had come up with winning bids now sat in a little clubroom with their proud teachers, and when Joe entered, what they saw was this: a handsome man with broad shoulders, skinny calves, tanned skin, suspiciously blonde hair, a slightly frayed hairline, a broad white grin, an extremely large nose, two sled-dog blue eyes centered in webs of white squint lines, a long, shiny, meat-colored scar across his right elbow and untied sneakers. The kids were not jocks; they were, for the most part, slouchy, brainy and quiet, and Joe took a seat next to a blonde girl who seemed to be the shyest of them all. For about two minutes, he spoke quietly to her, plying her with his smile; then he noticed Barnett across the table and said to the little girl, loudly, "Have you ever seen ears like those? Doesn't he look like a Doberman?" The little girl smiled but did not say anything. Joe folded his own ears forward. "Anybody have a knife?" he asked. "You can sharpen it on his ears."

Now, for a long time, I thought of Joe Montana as a "thinking man's quarterback," a "cerebral athlete" whose game — a greedy, hungry, gobbling thing, based miraculously on patience, restraint, even passivity — was an expression of some kind of Zen mastery. Naturally, when I first heard the story of the huddle in San Diego, I believed that Joe had made fun of Barnett's ears for calculated effect, to relax his team. I no longer think so. I have seen Joe and Tim Barnett together several times, and Joe has never *failed* to make fun of Barnett's ears. I am convinced that he cracked the joke in San Diego simply to get a laugh, just as I am convinced that — at the beginning of the last-minute 92-yard drive that beat the Cincinnati Bengals in the 1989 Super Bowl — he pointed out John Candy in the stands simply because he had *spotted* John Candy and wanted to share his find with his teammates. He is innocent of calculation. He is free of ulterior motive. He is unburdened by history. His Zen is not Eastern, but, rather, western Pennsylvanian. His Zen is the Zen not of the brainy but of the blessed.

"He isn't complicated," says Bill Walsh, the coach who presided over Joe's rise to professional glory. "People look for another agenda — It really isn't there. He just loves football. He loves to play the game. He plays with a smile on his face."

He plays with a smile on his face because in football he has found the magical alembic by which to turn the lead of his limitations into the gold of his legend. He loves football not because it frees him to create but because it constrains him to react, and he is very good at reacting. "A lot of people," he says, "try to do more than they're able to, than they are capable of. I don't." I once asked him if, during those famous moments of crunch time and crisis, when his team is behind and the clock is running, he tries especially hard to complete his first pass, because then he knows that the defense starts thinking, Oh, no, here comes Joe....And Joe answered that no, he tries to complete his first pass because it's always better to complete a pass than *not* to complete a pass. He feels the same way about the second pass, and the third. He is a simple man who plays a simple game, and "his simplicity," in the words of 49ers president Carmen Policy, "is his genius."

"He is able to operate on a simplistic level and come to decisions that others would think of as very complex," says Policy, who ought to know, because, in the most painful event in the history of the franchise, he traded Joe to the Chiefs, and admits that he was outwitted in the process. "It's like dealing with a person who walks into a crowded party and works the room and has everybody loving him. And you say 'How do you do that?' But it's nothing you can train for, not a muscle you can develop....It's not physiological. It's probably not even psychological. It's probably spiritual."

I have my own theory about Joe, of course. I have come to the conclusion that, at the moment of conception, Joe was spared the tiny whirring gear of doubt and introspection that at once hobbles, vexes and enriches our lives; I have come to believe that his mindset is a matter of circuitry, biology, evolution and destiny, and that when, at the end of this season, Joe Montana retires from football, he will become a fugitive from the very game — the very purpose — for which he was created.

·ε·

What, you haven't heard? He's retiring, after this, his sixteenth season in the NFL. Walking away at age 38. This is it, folks — the last campaign, the grand finale, the final episode of the Joe Show. No more perfection in desperation, no more final-second thievery, no more long passes when logic dictates that he should throw short, no more short passes when it's clear he absolutely must throw long, no more soft little flares that settle into a receiver's hands at the precise moment he is ready to run forever...no more Joe. Oh, sure, people have been talking about Joe retiring for *years*; now, however, *Joe* is talking about it, to his wife, Jennifer, to his parents, to his agent and friends, to other retired athletes, such as Roger Staubach and Reggie Jackson.... No, he won't come right out and say it, because he's always resented the sporting press's counsel in the matter of retirement, but he makes it clear that he wants to get out before he *has* to get out, before his last game turns out to be like last season's playoff in Buffalo, when the Bills clanged his head against the frozen turf and he sat on the sideline with a coat over his shoulders and nothing in his eyes, looking so pale, so *puny*.

"Oh, he has to," says Bill Walsh when asked about Joe's retirement. "You lose some of your quickness; you don't

THE GRIDIRON GAME

move and avoid people as well as you once did, and you start taking punishment."

Of course, Walsh is justified in his concern, because, as even Joe admits, Montana has taken some shots over the years...there have been a few injuries...well, a lot of injuries...indeed, enough traumatized tissue to warrant surgical invasion of Joe's body on a scale more often endured by medical-school cadavers.

"I thought after Buffalo that would be it, but he wasn't ready," says Joe's mother, Theresa Montana. "But I hope this is his last year, for his sake. He needs the rest." Yes, that's it, the kind of thing a mother says, and knows: that more than anything else, her son is tired. How long has he been playing football? For as long as Joe has been at his life, he has been at his game; his mother remembers him wearing out his grandfather, playing catch with him all day long, at age two. "He liked it," she says. "You and I walk down the street; Joe picks up a ball and starts playing just like you and I walk down the street."

He was born to play and raised to compete. He was an only child, and when his parents discovered within their son some great, hulking jones to win at whatever game he played, they did whatever was necessary to feed it. To give Joe a taste of pressure, his father, Joe Sr., exposed him to the best competition possible when Joe was seven or eight, driving the boy all over the state of Pennsylvania to play in basketball tournaments. To make sure that Joe had the whitest pants on his football team, his mother didn't just wash them, she *cleansed* them. "One day Joe came home and said 'Mom, I don't know how you do it but my pants are whiter than anyone else's.' I took him down to the basement and showed him the old-fashioned washboard. I said, 'This is how you do it. First soak 'em in cold water with a little bit of Tide. Then rub 'em. Then throw the water away and soak 'em in bleach and *hot* water. Then rub 'em again. *Then* throw them in the washer.' I didn't have the new kind of washing machine, either — I had the old-fashioned wringer when I was doing his clothes."

No wonder he's tired. Metaphorically, at least, he has been wearing the whitest pants on his team for virtually his entire life. In the little leagues...in high school...at Notre Dame...with San Francisco and now in Kansas City...he has always had this blinding *glow*; he has always been the great Joe Montana, and now, well, as his mother says, he needs a rest. The thing is, I don't think he's tired of wearing the whitest pants on the team; in fact, I think he *likes* wearing the whitest pants on the team. He's just tired of everyone else getting them dirty.

It's like some freaking bad dream. Joe doesn't want to wiggle, but he winds up wiggling anyway. He tries to tell the others that he doesn't want to wiggle, but they are too tall, or too beautiful, and they can't hear him. So he wiggles. He is on stage, with Brooks Robinson and Joe Willie Namath and Veronica Webb and Danny Manning and Miss U.S.A. and Dikembe Mutombo, in the basketball arena of the University of Arkansas, at a rally of Wal-Mart stockholders. The air smells vaguely of meat, and the stockholders are in full throat, demanding that the athletes and models do what they do, every morning, if they work in a Wal-Mart store; the Wal-Mart cheer. Joe is fourth in line; Joe is the hyphen, and the hyphen must wiggle. W! A! L! Now it's Joe's turn, so he drops into a kind of crouch and shakes his fanny as though he's performing an ethnic dance back in western

THE GRIDIRON GAME

Pennsylvania. The crowd roars its approval — *Joe!* — and later a goodly number of women approach and say, winkingly, "Nice wiggle, Joe."

In a limousine, he goes from the university's new basketball arena to its old one, where Hanes — a Wal-Mart vendor and one of the companies that pay Joe to license his name — has provided him a table at which he is to sign autographs. In anticipation of his arrival, a line has formed, a line that hums with the sound of America, that hums with appreciation of Joe.

"Is this the Joe line?"

"This is the Joe line."

"Joe!"

"Me and him — like *this*!"

Then a wife: "You have the patience to stand on line for an autograph, but you don't have the patience to stand on line with us when we're shopping?"

"Hey — It's *Joe*!"

"This man is *God*."

Then Joe comes in, and the wife fans herself. "Oh, is he a cutie. Oh, is he *cute*."

Joe is wearing a sharp olive-colored suit and his eyes are blue and steely. He is chewing a piece of gum, hard. He sits down at the table and begins signing black-and-white photos of himself. He smiles as he moves his pen across the photographs, but the smile is pickled and guarded, one per customer, and as he chews his gum, his jaw muscles grab his cheek like a claw.

The line moves. People ask Joe to sign jackets, footballs, and pennants, but he politely declines, because he can sign only licensed paraphernalia. People try to take pictures. "No pictures!" snaps a Hanes representative. A man asks Joe to sign two photographs. "Just one," Joe says.

"One?" the man says. "One." Joe says firmly. His eyes have a hunted look, and a vague air of resentment has settled over them. A man complains that Joe wouldn't sign his Canadian flag, and his wife says, "He's not friendly at all. He looks miserable."

As a matter of fact, he is. Joe knows that nobody at an autograph signing is getting what he wants. He knows that what the people want is a *moment* with Joe Montana, some little frisson of commonality, some indication that he *sees* them, and he knows that he has no moments to give. He is always gracious and always polite; he tries, however, to save his moments for his wife and four children. Quite often, his fans try to have some kind of moment with him when he is trying to have a moment with his children, and the result is a camera or a video camera thrust into the face of one of his little boys or girls, and Joe's miserable realization that his children have a better time in public places when Daddy stays home.

He would like to stay home, forever. He has never understood the intensity of public adulation, the sheer *need*. As a child, he never even had posters of athletes in his room, because he didn't want to watch or worship them, he wanted to *be* them; as an adult, he has always considered football merely a "fun job," and he really would have preferred playing it in empty stadiums, just him and the guys. In truth, the game he loves is already receding into the past, and his future is here, signing photographs of an old smile, among people who call him God and yet resent him for his distance, making money by learning how to wiggle.

ès

The plane rises slowly into the sky. I pray, because I am

THE GRIDIRON GAME

afraid of flying. Joe smiles, as is his habit. Joe has a dazzling smile, a theme he plays with variations. I assume, at first, that this is his interview smile — helpful, hopeful and eager-to-please, even in the face of impatience and befuddlement. I am asking him what he's going to do after he retires. Broadcasting? No, he is a positive person and can't imagine being paid to criticize his fellow ballplayers. Coaching? "Successful coaches tend to be players who can be satisfied succeeding through someone else. I'm too competitive for that. I can't stand not being in there." Politics? "Politics are too political." Books? "I started working on a book once, with a writer who probably would have done an excellent job — but it was so much time and effort." Business? "I'm not really a businessman, not yet. I feel like I don't know enough about the business world to make my own decisions."

No, what Joe dreams of is, in fact, what's making him smile; flight. He dreams of taking Jennifer and the children, with their billowing blonde hair, into his own airplane and then into the sky, away from the people who want him, who want them....He dreams of coming down, behind gates, behind fences, on a landing strip all his own, on a ranch all his own, and riding horses out to the grapes he grows, for the wine he makes, for the restaurant he runs, for the friends he has chosen, for the world he has created, all his own.

This is, of course, a rich man's dream, and Joe is, of course, a rich man. He is already taking flying lessons, searching for land in the Napa Valley and talking to winemakers about starting his own label, though "nothing too serious." He collects wine and is said to have discerning judgment. Joe has a "sensitive side," Jennifer Montana says, and she hopes, paradoxically, that the public will begin to appreciate it, once her husband gets out of football and regains his privacy. A lot of people have high hopes for Joe's retirement. His father hopes that he will compete on the senior golf tour. Bill Walsh hopes that he will coach. Roger Staubach hopes that he will go into business. I just hope that he doesn't turn into Joe DiMaggio, and so I ask him what he thinks people will be saying about him ten years from now, what he *wants* people to say about him ten years from now. We are flying. We are drinking wine. Joe is smiling.

"Oh, I don't know," he says. "How about 'Where is he?'"

I am listening to Joe talk about his trip to Brunei and wondering where greatness goes. Joe is in the Chiefs locker room with some of his teammates, and he is taking practice swings with an imaginary golf club and speaking about his host, the sultan's nephew, whom he calls Akeem. "Akeem didn't have to do shit," Joe says appreciatively. "When we played golf, he held out his foot and his valet tied his shoes. When he was ready to tee off, his valet put the ball on the tee. He didn't have to do *shit.*"

Where does greatness go? I have been following Joe to come up with some kind of answer. I have been following Joe to determine if greatness is, like a bus ticket, transferable, from *his* world, the world of football and holy innocence, to our world, the world of unholy complication...if it is indestructible, like matter, subject only to transformation, rather than extinction...or if it is as perishable as a perfect tomato, strictly of its moment, of *our* moment, and then gone. Now, however, I am thinking that Joe is trying to tell me something; that greatness goes wherever it wants to go; that it goes to Brunei, if the money is right; that it doesn't have to do shit. Then Joe's teammates leave, and I ask Joe a question of great concern. I am very superstitious, and the day is Friday the thirteenth. Severe thunderstorms are galloping in from the western plains, and I am scheduled to fly out of Kansas City at the same time they are scheduled to arrive. I ask Joe if, under the same conditions, he would get on the plane.

He smiles and looks me directly in the eye. He does not answer yes or no but instead leans forward as though telling me a secret, and says, "Friday the thirteenth? Thunderstorms? That just makes it *better*, doesn't it?"

I get on the plane two hours later. Like Tim Barnett in San Diego, and, for I all know, the sultan's nephew in Brunei, I have had my Joe Montana Moment. The plane rises quickly, easily; behind me, to the west, there is an insurrection of thunderheads, glowering like infidels. To the east, though, where I'm headed, the skies have been cleansed of all dark dreams, and greatness follows me home.

1994

Bill Plaschke

Doctor Provides a Shield for High School Athletes

It's a Friday afternoon, and this city's high school football MVP is making another big play.

This time it's a tackle, of a kid named Salvador Martinez, two hands on his shoulder pads that force him to remain on the tiny Crenshaw High bench.

While Martinez is down, Dr. Clarence Shields tenderly examines his stinging knee, calmly explains that it's only a bruise, applies a bag of ice.

Without a program founded by Shields, the injury is treated somewhat different.

It is not treated at all.

Before Shields, Martinez keeps playing, risking further damage. He limps home and tries to heal it the way an old wife would, maybe applying some balm, maybe soaking it in a hot bath of Epsom salts.

The next day, he limps into a local emergency room where he is surrounded by several other inner-city football players doing the same thing.

After waiting all morning for X-rays, he is seen by an emergency room physician who may not be well-versed in sports medicine.

At best, the player limps out with the bag of ice and simple advice that he should have been give 24 hours earlier.

At worst, the doctor misses a torn ligament that will make itself painfully evident a week later.

"Before," Martinez said, "you played until it hurt, then you kept playing until you couldn't stand it anymore."

And everybody played out of position. Coaches were trainers. Mothers were doctors. Children ignored their pain like men.

The came Shields, whose Team HEAL project has provided a sliver of hope during a football season clouded by death.

The program, jointly sponsored by the Los Angeles Orthopaedic Hospital Foundation and the Kerlan-Jobe Clinic, gives two high schools something missing from every other in the Los Angeles Unified School District.

Two certified, full-time, fully paid, on-site trainers who work with every sport.

Completely monitored physical exams of every athlete before football and basketball season.

A doctor at every football game. A doctor available for any serious injury in any sport.

While only Crenshaw and Dorsey are involved so far – "They are the two schools closest to my office," said Shields, who is not paid – he hopes to expand it when he finds more funding.

If this program was at Reseda High this year, who knows whether 18-year-old Eric Hoggat would have died shortly after his complaints of numbness during the game were

THE GRIDIRON GAME

not thoroughly checked.

"I've always said, it's very dangerous not to have more medical help on the sidelines," said Robert Garrett, Crenshaw football coach. "People need to understand this."

Until then, every city football game – including the current playoffs, which no longer involve Crenshaw or Dorsey – will begin with this question from the referee.

It involves the only assistance the players are guaranteed.

"Where's the paramedic? Rules say we can't start the game without a paramedic."

At a recent Crenshaw-Dorsey game, that question was posed to the Crenshaw sideline when Shields gently interrupted.

"It's OK. I'm a doctor," he said.

"You're a what?" said the referee.

Shields, small for someone with an impact so large, later shrugged.

"No doctors will come down here," he said. "Nobody cares about these kids, medically. Sometimes you wonder."

This Los Angeles native and longtime team doctor for the Rams was wondering the same thing two years ago when his team left town.

Having treated many neglected inner-city athletes for free during his Rams' tenure, Shields wondered what would happen with a little prevention.

"I saw so many kids whose chances at college scholarships and maybe even more were cut short because of injuries that could have been treated...I wondered why these kids shouldn't be given a better chance," he said.

One of those kids was a local running back who required major reconstructive knee surgery that could not have been properly treated in an emergency room.

Bill Plaschke

Shields fixed him with about $20,000 worth of free work, and the kid won a college scholarship worth far more than that.

One day after his senior season, the player visited Shields' office. "I wanted to give you something," the player said.

It was a thank-you card. Shields framed it, and set about forming Team HEAL, an acronym for Helping Enrich Athletes Lives.

Today the results can be witnessed in the varied duties of his two trainers, who are sponsored by HealthSouth physical therapy and rehabilitation centers.

Crenshaw's Warren Wood, a Brigham Young graduate who was far from his comfort zone in the inner city, has become the school safety net.

When Wood first arrived, the kids were so unfamiliar with trainers that when he treated them with ice, they ate it.

Dr. Clarence Shields, MVP for a second consecutive season, says he hopes this is only the beginning. For the children's sake.

1996

Pat Jordan
ଔ
Belittled Big Men

Daryl Bush, a Florida State University linebacker, reads the Bible every morning sitting on his bed beneath a poster of his girlfriend, a bikini-clad blonde who is a dancer with the school's Golden Girls at halftime. Dirty clothes are strewn on the bed across from him. "My roommate's clothes," says Bush, six feet two inches and 230 pounds. "The Jim Beam bottles on the shelf are his, too." Bush wants to make sure there is no misunderstanding about the dirty laundry (cleanliness is next to godliness), and especially not about the liquor bottles. He doesn't want to get in trouble with his coaches or the NCAA, since at 20 he is not old enough to drink in Florida.

Bush's teammates call him Psycho. He claims he doesn't know why, yet even in normal conversation his blue eyes glare with a barely restrained....what? Passion? Fury? He writes poetry in his spare time because he has "so much energy, I have to channel it by expressing myself." His poetry all has the same theme: bottled-up emotions that he tries desperately not to unleash until absolutely necessary. "I have an overwhelming desire to be my best," he says, which is why he plays football.

Over the last twenty years, his team, the Seminoles of Florida State University in Tallahasse, has won more regular-season games (171) and more postseason bowl games in a row (10) than any other team. The Seminoles won the national championship in 1993, have finished in the top four for the last eight seasons and are rated the eighth-best team in the country, with a 9 and 2 record. They'll get a chance to extend their record with their New Year's bowl game. But this status has not come without a price, and as is the case with all major college football programs, the price is paid by the players. They have to perform flawlessly on the field, in the classroom and in the public eye. They have to adhere to strict, often nonsensical NCAA rules. They have to produce national championships, which bring their schools millions of dollars and their coaches generous salaries. (Bobby Bowden, the Seminole coach, makes about $1 million a year.) If they expect to move up to "the next league," the NFL, their performances must be nearly perfect. So they build up their bodies with weightlifting. They develop an aggression suited to the playing field but ill-suited to life off it. They try to avoid the temptations of sex, drugs, alcohol, and illicit cash payments.

For years, Florida State players were more successful than most in not cracking under these pressures — until the late 1980s, when a series of scandals hit: a player was shot and killed, an ex-player was accused of being a drug kingpin. In 1994 three players in the span of nine days were arrested on sex-related charges; at the same time a report was published saying that a group of players had accepted cash and gifts from agents' representatives trying to curry their favor, in violation of NCAA rules.

Florida State is not alone among major college football programs when it comes to scandals. The University of Nebraska, last year's national champion, has on its team a player awaiting trial for attempted second-degree murder. Another recently pleaded no contest to misdemeanor charges for dragging a former girlfriend down three flights of stairs and is awaiting sentencing — and playing ball. The University of Miami has also had its problems with off-field misconduct, including a financial-aid scandal and publicity about drug use.

In fact, the Seminoles' problems are typical, except in one respect: Their coach, Bobby Bowden, is a born-again Christian whose stated goal is his players' "eternal salvation." Bowden prides himself on having a "clean team" and players whose success on the field glorifies God and is a testament to the players' and the coach's righteousness. Bowden's aspirations for his players make the Florida State football program a more extreme version than those of other schools, with the pressure to be devoutly Christian amplifying the pressure to be great.

One former Seminole, Terrell Buckley, now with the Miami Dolphins, says the glory that college athletes receive isn't enough compensation for what they have to go through: "They try to tell us how to walk. Don't do this. Don't. Don't. When you hear 'don't' so much, it's human nature to rebel. [They] make it seem like a business. Well, then we ought to treat it like a business." Jesus Hernandez, an offensive tackle with the Seminoles this year, says: "Everyone makes money but us. I hate the most that we don't get paid."

In the closing minutes of the third quarter, Florida State is on its home field battling Georgia Tech. Eighty thousand fans are chanting the Seminoles' war cry. They swing their hands forward in the tomahawk chop, their trademark. (Both chant and chop were adopted by Braves fans when Deion Sanders, the former Seminole cornerback, went to Atlanta to play some baseball.) A booming drum beats.

Bush and his defensive unit take the field. At the snap the Tech quarterback hands the ball off to his running back. The ball carrier bounces off one, two Florida linemen until out of nowhere, Bush drives his shoulder into the runner's gut with such force he seems to deflate. The football is dislodged; players from both teams dive for it. Florida's ball.

Bush rips off his helmet, his eyes wide and glassy. "Now we're having fun!" he screams. Football helps Bush release all those pressures football has created. "The pressure is not in performing," he says, "but in all the demands on my time."

Bush leaves his dormitory room at 8 a.m. every weekday to sign in for breakfast at Moore Athletic Center, even if he doesn't eat breakfast there. He steps outside into the fall air. The players' dormitory is set far apart from the rest of the student housing. Bush walks across the parking lot and says: "We have a cop patrolling every night. He makes sure no girls or sports agents knock on our doors."

Athletes like Bush have little contact with anyone outside their team. They and their coaches like it that way. The players disdain their fellow students for not being athletes, for not being dedicated and disciplined, and at Florida State, often for not being born-again Christians.

The coaches try to regiment every moment of the players' day; virtually the only sanctioned free time is Sunday and after games, which are held on Saturdays. The players' days are filled with classes; interviews with reporters (morning and afternoon sessions); meaningless check-ins for breakfast, lunch, and dinner (the players have their own

THE GRIDIRON GAME

dining area and the talk is always about football); team meetings, and practices, all designed essentially to bottle up their rising aggression until game day, when they can unleash it on their opponents. ("Basically," says Greg Frey, a lineman, "what we do is hit people for four years.") The coaches' control is also intended to insure that players don't break any of the arcane NCAA rules.

When a reporter invites Bush out for a meal, he panics. "I don't know," he says. "I have to check. Make sure it's legal." He finds out it is "legal," as long as he pays for his own meal. He mentions this three times to the waitress. "Separate checks," he says. "Make sure." He insists on leaving his own tip, which he places conspicuously on top of *his* bill. When a teammate is late picking him up for class, Bush refuses a reporter's offer of a ride because it is against NCAA rules. Even coaches, if they see a player walking in the rain, cannot give him a ride to class.

At Florida State, a player becomes ineligible when his grade point average falls below 2.0 for two consecutive semesters. Roger Grooters, the director of academic support services, says in his two and a half years at the school, no football player has flunked out. The team's graduation rate is 71 percent for players who entered the school in 1988 compared with 53 percent for players who entered in 1987.

While Bush is practicing, Potbelly's, a campus bar, is filled with handsome fraternity boys flirting with pretty sorority girls. Intellectual kids with shaved heads, earrings, and tiny sunglasses are snickering at the frat boys. A group of drunken alumni, here for the weekend game and an opportunity to relive their college days, sit at another table.

The football players never go to Potbelly's. The fraternity brothers might badger them about the game coming up. The intellectuals might make loud comments about "dumb jocks." The drunken alumni might try to goad them into a quarrel. So they hang together, like cops.

Before every game, the players are kept isolated until a few hours before kickoff. "It doesn't get much better than game day," says Bush. "There's no bigger thrill than hitting someone, beating them physically. When you hit someone and take control of them, you can see the fear in their eyes. The only fear I have is injury. I hurt my knee recently and missed a few games. It made me realize I wasn't invincible. So I began to play more relentlessly. I took hold of that fear because there's always the chance I might never play again."

Not all Florida State football recruits can "take hold" of that fear, says Randy Oravetz, the university's trainer. He says that when freshmen arrive, "they feel pressured to play with pain," adding that some "can't raise their pain threshold to the college level and push through it."

On an October afternoon, Warrick Dunn, the Seminole tailback who is one of the team's Heisman Trophy candidates, is wrestling with avoiding pain and playing with injury. Sitting on a cot in the trainer's room at halftime of the Florida State-Wake Forest game, he points to his arm and says in a barely audible voice, "It hurts up here." Oravetz applies an ice pack. "No, higher," Dunn says.

"I hate to get hit," says Dunn, who at five feet nine inches and 178 pounds looks too slight to play football. "I never lower my head to hit the other guy. I try to bounce off him, not run through him."

Dunn wants an NFL contract that will provide financial security for himself and his family. But NFL scouts have told him he might be too susceptible to injury to play in "the next league."

So when Dunn leaves the trainer's room to start the second half against Wake Forest and a teammate asks him how his arm is, Dunn shakes his head. But still, he will play this half. Bowden wants him to run for at least 100 yards this game to enhance his Heisman Trophy chances. And Dunn has to play to prove he is not injury-prone.

ે∙

Scott Bently looks like Jay Gatsby. Tall, slim, handsome, with straight blond hair that would fall over his eyes if not for the baseball cap he always wear around campus, pulled low over his forehead so no one will know him.

When Bentley enters a game to kick a field goal, Seminole fans boo him. When he misses, they boo louder. Bowden, on the sidelines, kicks dirt and mutters, "Kick the damned ball right!" Bentley trots back to the sidelines, head down, and stands apart from his teammates with his helmet on. He begins to pantomime kicking that missed field goal over and over, his leg high above his head like a Rockette.

In 1993, Bentley, who grew up in Aurora, Colorado, was Florida State's most celebrated recruit. His picture was on the cover of *Sports Illustrated* before he ever kicked a ball for the Seminoles. Bowden said he would be the key to the team's winning a national championship that year. In 1991 and 1992, Florida State had lost its chance for the championship by losing games to the University of Miami by one point each when its kicker missed a goal in the closing minutes.

"My dad wanted me to go to his alma mater, Notre Dame," Bentley says. But Bentley believed Bowden when he said he was "the final piece to the puzzle to win the national championship."

On January 1, 1994, in his freshman year, Bentley trotted onto the field at the Orange Bowl in Miami with 21 seconds left in a game the University of Nebraska was leading, 16-15. Bentley faced the ball on the 22-yard line. "I was like on an island," he says. "I couldn't hide. The whole world would see me mess up." When Bentley strode toward the ball and swung his leg in a right-left arc, Bowden put his hands over his eyes. After the kick, he said to Bentley, "I knew you'd get one sometime."

"Everyone said that's why I was at FSU," says Bentley. "And I did it. I won Coach Bowden's first national championship."

That spring, Bentley had a sexual encounter with a girl, which he audiotaped to protect himself, he says, because "my teammates had warned me she would get back at you if you got her mad." Then he played the tape for some teammates. She filed charges. Bentley was arrested for interception of aural communication. He pleaded no contest, performed community service, and was suspended from the team during the summer. He was reinstated again in the fall, but when he missed two field goals in a game against Clemson, he was benched for the rest of the season.

"I was devastated," he says. "I think they were punishing me for the sex thing. I felt like a complete failure."

Bentley's roommate, Danny Kanell, is also tall and handsome. But he looks more like Tom Sawyer than Gatsby. He walks around campus with the blissed-out smile of someone who has absolute certitude about his life.

Kanell was the second-string quarterback who held the ball for Bentley's winning field goal in the Orange Bowl. He is Florida State's record-breaking quarterback, one of the four best in the country, the team's other Heisman Trophy candidate. He seems always to have a Bible in his hand and says he reads it for at least twenty minutes every day to ward off temptations. "Girls will do anything for football players," he says. "Guys always want to challenge us to fight. Agents are always calling, like putting candy in front of our faces." Kanell is perhaps less vulnerable than most of his teammates to some temptations. His father, Dan, is an orthopedic surgeon and the Miami Dolphins' team physician. Danny drives a $30,000 Toyota 4-Runner around campus.

Though Kanell, a senior, became the team's starting quarterback in the 1994 season, he says he still fears standing in the backfield to pass while "six guys are coming at your throat to knock your head off" and adds, "It's chaos around you. Someone's hand in your face. Thing going so fast. I'd be shaking in my shoes."

When Bentley and Kanell first roomed together in Bentley's freshman year, they became close friends. Kanell held the football for Bentley for the *Sports Illustrated* cover. When Bentley was about to kick the field goal in the Orange Bowl, Kanell said, "When you make it, jump into my arms so I'll be on TV, too." Bently did. Today, however, though they are still roommates, they no longer hang out together. A player who requested anonymity says maybe it is because Bentley was the Florida State hero as a freshman, but now Kanell has overshadowed him. He adds that Kanell thinks Bentley has a complex about him, that Bentley tried to steal his girlfriends. Which is an odd complaint from a youth who claims he prays every day to ward off the temptation of the flesh. The same player says he thinks Kanell's religious activities are for public consumption, not done out of a private conviction. (Kanell gives sermons at churches to youngsters about the evils of drugs and alcohol.)

Today, Kanell hears mostly cheers from Florida State fans, even when one of his passes is intercepted. Bentley hears mostly boos — he's in a kicking slump, and he embarrassed "the program." But he is expected to perform despite the pressure. "Scott said he feels like he's kicking against 80,000 FSU fans," says Kanell, smiling. "I told him, 'That's why Coach Bowden recruited you.'"

※

It is almost midnight after the Wake Forest game. The stadium is dark. The players have all left with their girlfriends and families. Everyone's gone except a lone figure crossing the street, heading for the stairs that lead to the players' dormitory up a hill. The dark figure is Enzo Armella, short and bulky with a bull neck. He steps onto the first step and swings his left leg up after him. He steps onto the next step and swings his left leg up. He moves painfully up the flight of stairs.

Armella was never afraid of pain or injury when he played on the Seminoles' defensive line a year ago. "I was a mean player," he says. "No one ran up the middle on me. I was a bad guy. I thought I was tougher than anyone else."

Armella, who was raised in Miami, remembers experiencing "culture shock" when he got to the university: "Coach Bowden made us go to these white and black Baptist churches. People were yelling 'Amen!' and jumping up and down. I went with the flow. I never missed chapel but once, and you know what? The next game I blew out my leg."

It was parents' weekend, September 24, 1994, in Armella's junior year. He was pursuing a University of North Carolina receiver about to catch a screen pass, when one of his own teammates speared him in the leg with his helmet. "It was the worst pain I ever felt," Armella says. He was carried off the field on a stretcher while Florida State fans cheered him. He had surgery to repair ligament and nerve damage in his left leg, but it wasn't successful. He still walks with what he calls "a dropped foot." He needs another operation to transplant nerves and muscles if he ever expects to walk normally again.

"I was devastated," he says. "My career was over."

Jesus Hernandez was a boy of 9 in 1980 when he sat between his mother's knees on a small boat filled with two hundred refugees fleeing Cuba for Miami during the Mariel boatlift. Today he is a mammoth man, six feet two inches, 297 pounds of startling, dark handsomeness that always seems to take women's breath away.

When Hernandez arrived, he was shocked, he says, by the amount of pressure from coaches and peers to win. "You can't sleep after a bad practice," he says. "In class, you're thinking about how you messed up. You have to do better or you won't play. It could lead to the good life in the NFL. So you develop this tough-guy attitude. You think you're invincible. Then you remember what happened to Pablo and it's a reality check."

Pablo Lopez, also from Miami, arrived at Florida State to begin his freshman year in 1983 as a six-foot-four-inch, 240-pound offensive lineman. Two years later, he had added forty pounds of muscle to his frame and had acquired an aggressive attitude. He like to hang out with his teammate Ed Clark, a linebacker who, according to one of his coaches, "was a fighter."

On September 13, 1986, while hundreds of students were milling about outside a gymnasium where a fraternity-sponsored dance was being held, Clark happened to drive by. One of a group of townies kicked Clark's car, and words were exchanged. Lopez saw what was happening and walked over to check on his friend. At one point, Clark waved a pistol around, and the townies left. They returned in the car an hour later with a shotgun stowed in the trunk and parked behind the gym.

Clark, still angry over the car-kicking incident, walked with Lopez over to the townies and punched one of them. The other man, Byron Christopher Johnson, a five-foot-ten-inch, 160-pound short-order cook, immediately pulled the shotgun from the trunk and pointed it at Lopez, who took a few steps toward Johnson and shouted, "You don't have the heart to shoot me!" Johnson fired; Lopez fell and then died on the way to a hospital. Shortly after his death, Florida State lost a crucial game to the University of Nebraska. Bowden said at the time: "We lost Pablo, and we lost our best lineman, to be honest. It might have made a big difference had we not lost Pablo."

Lopez wasn't the last Florida State football recruit whose macho attitude got him into trouble. Randy Moss, a six-foot-four-inch, 180-pound wide receiver from Rand, West Virginia, lost a scholarship to Notre Dame because, he says, "in high school, one of my home boys took it out on a white boy who'd written some racial things. When the dude was on the ground, I kicked him."

Moss was arrested and plea-bargained his felony charge down to two counts of misdemeanor battery. He served three days in jail.

He appeared to be damaged goods until the Notre Dame coach, Lou Holtz, a longtime friend of Bowden, recommended he accept Moss. When Bowden was asked by reporters why he accepted a player with Moss's background, he said, "Trust me. I found out what a good kid he was."

※

In the afternoon, before practice, Bowden likes to walk

alone, halfway up the university's deserted home stadium. He says he needs that time by himself to "clear his head." He may well need that time because of all his activities beyond the stadium, which he spends more time on than most college coaches do.

He sells himself and Florida State nonstop, seven days a week. He gives speeches to civic groups, business people, teachers, coaches, at conventions, at sports-card shows. Sunday mornings, after he tapes his television show, after a breakfast answering reporters' questions about Saturday's game, he often hurries off to give a sermon at a local church. On Thursday evenings, Bowden broadcasts his radio show from the Buffalo Connection restaurant near the campus. The restaurant is mostly filled with families, since virtually all Tallahasseans are Seminole fans. They wait patiently for Bowden to pose with them for pictures or to sign posters of himself.

Just about every day, after practice, Bowden sits in the lobby of the athletic center and answers questions from reporters. He has always been accessible to the press, he says, because "we are in the selling business and we need the press."

He is paid to endorse Nike athletic merchandise, Lykes hot dogs, Bobby Bowden's Seminole football camp, Ford automobiles. Before all home games, during halftime and after the games, the public-address announcer reminds fans to watch Boden's TV show, listen to his radio show, buy the Ford cars he recommends. Bowden was even paid $50,000 by a sports writer, Ben Brown, for unlimited access to the Seminoles for Brown's book, *Saint Bobby and the Barbarians*.

Last April, Bowden's lawyer wrote a letter to Florida State's athletic director, Dave Hart, in an attempt to negotiate a "lifetime" agreement for the coach, saying the Bowden "brought the football program from the brink of disaster to the position it enjoys today as one of the top programs in the country." To retain Bowden's services, the lawyer suggested the school give Bowden a base salary and various supplements totaling well over $1 million. The coach wound up with a $150,000 base salary, a $225,00 salary supplement from Nike for endorsements, $275,000 for media programs, $200,000 for speeches, a $100,00 annuity, and a $25,000 life insurance payment. His five-year contract awards him $975,000 a year.

For years, Bowden was underpaid at Florida State compared with other major college coaches. But now, approaching retirement, he sees that money simply as the gold star on his coaching exam. "It's a matter of pride," he says.

Bowden is not unaware of how his salary demands appear to his players, without whom he couldn't make those demands. "My boys are reminded daily that they bring in huge sums of money for FSU," he says — $11.5 million a year, to be exact. "That's why I recommended that all college football players be paid for playing. I recommended to the NCAA they be paid $75 a month."

At practice, sitting high up in the bleachers, Bowden watches the players below like God as personified during the Industrial Revolution, a great clockmaker who simply taps the pendulum once to begin time.

His son, Jeff, an assistant coach of the team, says: "He leaves the coaching to his assistants. He doesn't care what we do as long as we get the ball in the end zone." Chuck Amato, assistant head coach, says that the assistant coaches formulate each game plan and that "Coach Bowden doesn't know what we're going to do." The only time Bowden intrudes in a game, says Amato, is when it's close in the final minutes. In one game against Penn State, Bowden wondered why Penn State opted to go for a two-point conversion after each of two touchdowns, until Amato explained the strategy. "Oh, that's why," said Bowden. And Bowden's legendary recruiting skills are brought into play only after his coaches have scouted a prospect. "Coach Bowden recruits who we tell him to," says Amato.

Before the game with Georgia Tech, the high school recruits are standing along the Florida State sidelines, watching the two teams do calisthenics at opposite ends of the field. The white recruits are tall, thin quarterbacks and linebackers. The black recruits are huge, big-bellied lineman and tiny, trim, wide receivers. All recruits are accompanied by student hostesses called Garnet and Gold Girls.

One pretty hostess looks up at a huge recruit and says, "So you're a tackle?"

The recruit smiles sheepishly and looks down at his feet.

"You're sooo big!" she says with wide-eyed wonder. Then she reaches up a languid hand with long, red fingernails and lays it seductively on his shoulder. The hint of a promise she will never have to keep.

Most black players at Florida State, which has a mostly white student population, don't date fellow students. They date girls from Florida A&M University, the predominantly black college that lies alongside Florida State.

Kamari Charlton, an offensive tight end, who is from the Bahamas, dates an A&M girl. When they go out on her campus, he says, "FAMU girls come up to me and say I sold out by going to white FSU. I say my being here is not a black-white issue. I don't see black and white. I never experienced racism in *my* country."

At Florida State, Charlton has always considered himself "a loner." He used to chafe at his coaches' constant reminder never to embarrass "the program." He says, "It was like being under a constant microscope." When he tried to break up with his girlfriend one night, she pleaded with him not to. Then they had sex. The following morning he found himself in jail, charged with sexual battery.

Charlton was suspended from school in June 1994 and went on trial that fall. He was acquitted of all charges after less than two hours of jury deliberation. "Everyone said I had embarrassed the program. I said, 'Forget the program. This is my life. I embarrassed *myself*.' The program, the program."

Forrest Conoly, a six-foot-six-inch, 328-pound offensive tackle, also embarrassed "the program" last year. He was one of a group of Florida State players involved in the so-called Foot Lacker Scandal, which earned the university the nickname Free Shoes U. and an NCAA inquiry yet to be completed. On a Sunday in 1993, a Las Vegas freelance agent not registered in Florida paid for $6,000 worth of sports merchandise (sneakers, caps, sweatsuits) for a group of football players at a Foot Locker store.

"Oh, when it rains, it pours!" wailed Bowden at the time. He was referring not only to the Foot Locker incident but also to the fact that two of his players (Bentley and Charlton) and one of his ex-players (Sean Jackson, a tailback) had just been arrested on sex-related charges. Jackson had exposed himself to a 22-year-old female student and asked her to perform a sex act on him. He pleaded no contest.

As if that were not enough, Corey Sawyer, a cornerback, was discovered to have bought a new $30,000 Nissan Pathfinder only days before the Orange Bowl game. Sawyer claimed he got the money from his mother, Lydia Clark, a part-time cashier at a school in Key West. She told reporters she earned $8.22 an hour. (Sawyer now plays for the Cincinnati Bengals.)

☙

Before the Wake Forest game, the players assemble in the weight room for the chapel service. They're handed prayer cards for today's sermon. They move silently, big, hulking men in their shoulder pads and padded pants, while Clint Purvis, team chaplain, stands in their midst and searches for the spotlight. He moves a little to his left until he feels the overhead fluorescent light bathe him in a surreal orange glow. Finally, he begins:

"I want to talk to you today about Jesus Christ when he spoke to his team at the Last Supper. He told them he was proud of them but they'd have to play the game without him. Walking out of that locker room to the field, he said: 'I'm the true vine and every branch will bear fruit, but no branch will bear fruit by itself unless it remains on the vine. You'll bear much fruit if you remain on the vine with me.' This is like Coach Bowden telling you what you have to do on offense and defense....Now remember, your coaches love you. The greatest thing you can do for them is to play the best you can and then say: 'God made that tackle, not me, because I am connected to the vine. I will produce fruit and give glory to God.'"

After their days at Florida State, a select number of players will "give glory to God" on the NFL playing fields. In the 1994-95 season, eleven players were drafted into the league. Eight of those draftees remain. Grooters, the director of academic support services, acknowledges that "some kids don't have it all together when they leave here. I know of a few who are doing nothing now with their lives." Yet many former Florida State players who learned to deal with the pressure of big-time college football used what they had learned and took jobs in business, law enforcement, or the criminal justice system. Others did not fare as well. One graduate was just arrested on state and federal drug charges. He faces a thirty-two-count federal indictment.

As Bowden enters yet another locker room for his usual pregame pep talk, the players assemble around him. They sit while he stands, shuffling his feet, chewing gum, his eyes shaded by sunglasses. "Today I saw some of y'all struttin' in warm-ups like cool cats," he says. "There's no place in football for cool cats. Football needs intense people. I want you to tire them out. Fatigue makes cowards of men. You won't dominate them unless you're mean."

1995

Tim Green
From The Dark Side of the Game

Taking the needle is something NFL players are proud to have done. It is a badge of honor, not unlike the military's Purple Heart. It means you were in the middle of the action and you took a hit. Taking the needle in the NFL also lets everyone know that you'd do anything to play the game. It demonstrates the complete disregard for one's well-being that is admired in the NFL between players.

There are obvious physiological reasons for pain. Pain lets us know that something is wrong. We have injured our bodies in a way that demands attention. Pain is a warning to proceed with care, that more damage is imminent if the dangerous activity is not curtailed or arrested altogether. Novocain or Xylocaine, or whatever kind of -caines the doctors use to numb the human body, is a prevalent part of life in the NFL. As I said, players admire peers who take a shot of Xylocaine before a game. It is a certain sign of toughness and lets everyone know that that player can be counted on to "do whatever it takes."

I would have taken a needle. I even tried to get one once. The time I separated my collarbone, I begged for the needle. There were only five weeks to go in the season, and I was in the last year of my first contract. Each of the prior three years I'd spent time on injured reserve. I knew that it was essential for me to play despite the separated bone if I was to avoid the permanent stigma of being injury-prone. The pain was severe and I was going to play no matter what. So, I reasoned, why not take a needle and make it manageable? The team doctors wouldn't give it to me though. They said the area in question was too close to my heart and lungs to risk injecting the drug.

In one way, I am ashamed to say I never took a needle. I never got to show my teammates that I would make what is thought of as the ultimate sacrifice for the good of the team. Now that life in the NFL is behind me I could proclaim with condescension that I was too smart to have allowed something like that to happen to me, that I saw the big picture and that certainly I knew playing in one game of football wasn't worth the real risk of permanent and serious injury to my body. But if I said that, and acted like that, I would be lying. I wasn't that smart, even though I knew the story of someone who took the needle and will pay for it for the rest of his days.

The Falcons had a safety in the late 1980s whose name was Bret Clark. Bret was an All-America from Nebraska who had taken the route to the NFL through the USFL, which was fairly common at that time. He was one of the players who got more money for playing in the now defunct league than he was being offered by NFL teams. During his final NFL season Bret injured his knee.

Now you have to know a little bit about knee injuries

before we go on. Most doctors will admit that the real extent of a knee injury is uncertain until they actually open you up with a knife and go inside. Even with the advent of the MRI, which is supposed to give doctors an accurate three-dimensional image of the inside of the knee, things are still quite uncertain. In the late 1980s, before MRIs were in vogue, there were three ways physicians could evaluate the damage done to an injured knee.

First, there was, and still is, the manual manipulation of the joint to test for pain and loose ligaments. I can tell you that I've seen doctors proclaim players to be perfectly fine after one of these examinations when it was ultimately discovered that the player's entire knee was destroyed. When I say destroyed, I mean "The Terrible Triad" where the anterior cruciate ligament, the medial collateral ligament, and the cartilage have all been torn. I've also seen it go the other way, where the doctor determined that the knee was ruined and subsequently found to be merely sprained or bruised. Second, there was a procedure called an arthrogram, where the knee was injected with dye and then X-rayed. To the layman, the accuracy of this procedure seemed to be dubious at best. Finally, a doctor might have chosen to do an exploration with an arthroscope, which was a surgical invasion but would give the best indication of what was really going on inside the joint.

It was by one of the aforementioned methods that it was determined Bret Clark had damaged the cartilage in his knee. It was also determined that he could continue to play despite the pain and difficulty he had in even walking on his knee. At first, Bret would try to practice, using ice and anti-inflammatories to battle the imminent swelling from putting that kind of strain on his already damaged joint. At the end of the week, on Sunday mornings, his knee would be drained.

If you have never had your knee drained, you should know that it's not as easy as turning on the tap of a keg and letting the contents spill out. When a knee fills with fluid, it looks like a puffy grapefruit. When you touch it, it squashes, not unlike a miniature waterbed. That fluid, one of the body's protections against overusing an injured joint, prevents the full range of motion, which disables the person from running or even walking without a limp. To extract this pale, clear yellow fluid, a large needle (this horse needle seems no smaller than a cocktail straw when it's going in your knee) is inserted in the side of your knee and forced deep into the joint, all the way under your kneecap. The pain is excruciating. The plunger is extracted and, like a fat plastic mosquito, the syringe slowly bubbles as it is filled with the yellow fluid, which is sometimes swirling with diluted crimson clouds of blood. Bret would have this done every Sunday. And then, immediately after the draining, smaller needles would be used to strategically inject the Xylocaine that would mercifully numb his knee.

As the weeks passed, his limp during the week became more pronounced. He would practice less and less, until finally he didn't practice at all. Bret would sit in the meetings and absorb all he could about what was going to happen. He would have to mentally run through practice reps that backup players would actually perform. He could play without practicing. He was that good. He took the needle every week. He was that tough. Everyone marveled at the pain and obvious physical damage this young man endured in the name of winning. He was a team player, an example to us all.

Then, one Sunday morning, the horse needle produced nothing more than a viscous red goop. With no fluid coming out, the swelling could no longer be controlled. Although Bret took the needle once again and tried to gimp out there with the rest of the team, it was no use. The swelling in the joint would not permit him to perform. His body had finally defeated the wiles of modern medicine.

That was the end of Bret Clark's career. He was finished with the NFL and the NFL was finished with him. They operated and tried to clean up the mess, but his knee was already ruined. The cartilage that was causing the swelling in his knee week after week was torn. Like a loose flake of metal in a gear box, the rest of the joint slowly but surely degenerated, grinding itself down into useless gears.

The last I heard of Bret was that he was living somewhere in suburbia with his wife and kids. His knee will always be a problem. The teammate who spoke to him told me that he was having trouble just playing in the front lawn with the kids. I wonder when he explains to them what happened how he will describe it. I wonder if his Purple Heart leaves him feeling proud, or despondent.

ଏ⭐

The Best and Worst Places to Play in the NFL

When players talk about NFL stadiums they're not concerned with cushioned seats or plenty of peanuts for the fans. Players are preoccupied with the atmosphere. This means the type of crowd, the condition of the field, the feel of the tunnels, the locker room, and the landscape.

BUFFALO

The strangest place to go as a player is Buffalo. It's like landing on a different planet and being welcomed (or unwelcomed) by an alien nation. Your bus takes you from downtown Buffalo along the edge of Lake Erie and out to the suburbs where the stadium is. During that ride, you pass enormous old mills, warehouses, and factories. Most of these are nothing more than hulking abandoned shells, like the burnt-out destroyed spacecraft of an earlier invasion by a gigantic race that failed just as you too will surely fail. It's hard to win in Buffalo.

Every time I've been there, the very sky has been otherworldly, dark, ominous, billowing piles of gray smoke stacked for miles above you, obliterating even a hint of sun, another harbinger of the defeat to come.

When your bus nears the stadium, you notice that the roadways are lined with strange humanoid forms, bare to their waists, with red- and blue-colored skin carelessly exposed to the unkind elements. They shriek at you to go home. They spit. They throw cups of beer. They make wildly obscene signs with their hands, mouths, and feet. As the stadium comes into view, so does a regiment of Buffalo's finest: aerodynamic homes that move, spacecraft sprouting antennae and flying brazen flags of red and blue in the cold wind. Outside these craft, open pits burn out of control, searing meat of unknown origin as it slowly turns on metal spits. More aliens shriek. They wail. Go home. You'd like nothing more. But now it's too late and they feed you to their team. The Bills grind you up like a crude sausage machine. The crowd jeers. It begins to rain. You look at the clock and think about a warm bath at home, eight hundred miles away, on a different planet.

PHILADELPHIA

Philadelphia is known by almost every player in the league as the most hostile place to play. The crowds there make the Buffalo people seem like troops of Boy Scouts. Their mouths are so foul and so loquacious that they could make whores blush. The field too is the most inhospitable in the league. Seams crisscross the artificial surface like poorly disguised jungle booby traps.

CHICAGO

Soldier Field is the stuff dreams are made of. The neoclassical columns and friezes that rise up from behind the excited crowds transport you to the days of Rome when gladiator slaves battled to win the right to be free men. The turf is in fact turf. It smells like a freshly cut back lawn on a summer morning. The wind is always a factor. The team plays hard and mean, but they're the type of guys who would take you out for a beer after the contest, if such a tradition was cultivated by the NFL. Across the street is the Field Museum. On the other side is the water's edge, Lake Michigan, the Shedd Aquarium, and the city's planetarium. This stadium is a true civic center and if they ever move the Bears' playing site to the suburbs or inside a dome, Mike McCaskey should be run out of town on a rail.

SAN FRANCISCO

The disturbing thing about San Francisco is the type of fan they attract. The tickets for these events are among the costliest in the league. People who own season passes to these coveted events are as likely to have two or three degrees hanging on the den wall at home as one. It is an educated and well-to-do crowd. This is disturbing because of the way they behave, like maniacs. Crude and rude. You can be sure to hear taunting from the people in the front row on the fifty-yard line. Their comments may not be as vile as the ones you hear in Philadelphia, but what the San Francisco crowd lacks in depravity, they make up for with relentlessness. There's something truly unsettling about having a high-tech executive dressed in a button-down Ralph Lauren shirt with a matching sweater slung around his shoulders screaming with red-faced ire, "Green, you suck!"

Rest at ease though, once outside the stadium walls these same fans revert to mild-mannered Americans. I once ventured out into the parking lot after a game to purchase a six-pack of beer for the bus ride to the airport from some tailgaters, and I was treated like the prodigal son. They refused my money, and sent me back to the bus laden not only with cold beer, but sandwiches and polite wishes of good luck for the rest of the season.

THE MEADOWLANDS

Football in a can. This is no stadium, it's a facility. It's set in the middle of the swamps outside Newark, New Jersey, that is. The neighborhood is a Superfund nightmare. The grass is plastic. The rain is dirty. During Giants games, some fans wear Jets colors. During Jets games some fans wear Giants colors. Curse the Giants for ever leaving Yankee Stadium. This place reminds me of a disposable razor. I can't wait until they throw it away. Go home to New York, both of you.

CLEVELAND

Here's a place you don't mind getting shouted at. It's what you expect from the fans in Cleveland. Drive through the city and outside the wonderfully Gothic downtown square and you'll see factories that belch real fire from their stacks. The stadium itself is rundown. The water pressure in the showers is worse than at a mountain campsite. The locker room is crowded. The steel of the structure is rusted. The concrete is damp. The field, although meritoriously grass, comes up in clumps the size of a large pizza. Dog biscuits rain down on your helmet from the end zone area known as "The Dog Pound." That's okay. You wouldn't expect anything less. Again, wind and clouds and sometimes rain or even snow are part of the experience. This is football for real people.

ANAHEIM

God bless St. Louis. I can even forgive their dome. Anaheim was no place to play football. It was a baseball stadium. The sun always shined. The crowds were anemic. Smog hung in the air like the must of an attic. Once the plumbing backed up during the game and afterward there was six inches of raw sewage on the locker room floor. I don't have to say it.

GREEN BAY

This is the kind of place where people stand quietly before the national anthem and then sing. There is no wild cheering until the last words of the song have ceased to echo. This is the kind of place that claps politely when an opposing player is carried off the field. Instead of hot dogs, people eat brats with mustard. Going to Green Bay is like stepping forty years back in time. It's a pleasure.

MILE HIGH

Here too the people are like the neighbors in a small town during the holidays. They wear the colors of the team, a sea of orange and blue. The elevation is so high that it feels like someone sucked the air from your lungs with an industrial vacuum. Just running out onto the field from the sideline makes you delirious, so it's hard to appreciate the lovely snowcapped mountain range in the distance beyond the stadium walls.

RFK

This stadium is set on the wrong side of the tracks in D.C. with the highway on one side and the tenements on the other. That whole end of town is getting rundown and the stadium isn't immune from the blight.

The concrete tunnels ooze dank slime. That's okay. The field is grass. Even the tightest coach in the league will let his players have a few hours the day before the game to see the memorials. Most teams stay at the L'Enfante Plaza, and the ride to the stadium from there takes you through the European architecture of our country's capital in all its grandeur, past the Smithsonian, the Capitol, and the Supreme Court. You can feel the power.

DOMES

If you've been to one, you've been to them all.

1996

Reprinted by permission of Warner Books, Inc. New York, New York, U.S.A. From *The Dark Side of the Game* by Tim Green. Copyright © 1996 by Tim Green. All rights reserved.

Rick Lipsey

How Zebras Get Their Stripes

During a Chicago Bears-Detroit Lions game at Soldier Field in 1972, referee Norm Schachter told Bears linebacker Dick Butkus that if he didn't lay off Lions quarterback Greg Landry, Schachter would penalize him for roughing the passer. Butkus went ballistic, kicking dirt, spitting, cussing and waving his finger at Schachter. For a few plays Schachter let Butkus vent his ire. Finally Schachter said, "If you don't shutup, I'll bite your head off."

"Go right ahead," Butkus said with a snort. "Then you'll have more brains in your stomach than you do in your head."

Wrong, Dick. Contrary to popular opinion, NFL officials aren't dumber than coaches, players and fans. In fact, they may be the smartest guys on the field. Officiating in the NFL is no weekend hobby for football dilettantes.

A high-profile, high-pressure career isn't a prerequisite for carrying an NFL whistle, but it certainly helps. Monday through Friday, umpire Jim Quirk, a nine-year veteran of officiating, sells U.S. government securities as a senior vice president at Sanwa Securities in New York City. Quirk, 56, makes transactions worth anywhere from a few million to a half-billion dollars at a time, dozens of times a day. In his office — a desk on Sanwa's frenetic trading floor — are four phones, a computer, order sheets, financial journals and an NFL rule book.

"Guys making calls in the NFL usually have intense careers that involve lots of tough decision-making," says Quirk. "As a trader, if you don't react with authority, you'll get steamrollered — and go broke. It's the same deal in the NFL. If you don't think and act like you're the best, the man in control, you'll get crucified."

The NFL employs 112 officials, recruited from among the best 50,000 refs who work in organized football every year. No unsolicited applications, please. "If somebody is worthy of working for us, we'll go after him," says Jerry Seeman, the league's director of officiating and himself a former NFL ref with 16 years on-field experience.

The league has 50 scouts who hunt for new blood in Division I and I-AA college conferences. Each fall the scouts keep close tabs on about 150 college officials, each of whom needs at least five years in a conference to qualify. That number is whittled to 15 in the off-season. Candidates give the league details of their officiating and of their personal and employment histories. Then they come to New York City for a two-hour interview with the three NFL supervisors at league headquarters. Finally the league gives them rigorous psychological exams and makes background checks. The NFL's 40-man private investigation arm, made up mostly of former FBI agents, interviews friends, neighbors and coworkers of the prospective officials, looking for any history of gambling, drinking or unsavory associations.

From the group of 15 candidates the league usually hires

six new whistle-blowers each year to replace retiring officials and the few who are fired. The pay is generous. In the regular season officials earn $1,325 to $4,009 per game, depending on experience. Playoff games pay $9,800 and the Super Bowl, $11,900. The weekly travel benefits include first-class airfare, concierge-level hotel rooms and a per diem of $205 for the first night and $155 for the second. Upon retirement officials receive a pension of $150 a month for each year of service, provided that they have worked at least 10 years.

But it's not the money that attracts guys to NFL officiating. It's the thrill of being part of the country's most popular professional sports league. "At first I was awed by it all," says Red Cashion, 64, a 24-year veteran of NFL refereeing and the chairman emeritus of ANCO Insurance, a company he cofounded in Texas in 1955. But the enormity of it all makes you work that much harder."

Most officials say that they devote more time during the season to the NFL than to their full-time jobs. Almost daily they review game tapes, study the 134-page rule book and talk on the phone with other officials and staff members at the league office. Once a week they do a take-home rules exam that is not graded but is meant to keep them sharp. Most refs also work out daily, running and doing various types of cardiovascular exercise. That adds up to about 25 hours a week.

Each game takes another two days of their time. Officials must arrive in town by noon the day before a game for the weekly crew meeting. On Aug. 31 the crew working the opening-day game between the San Francisco 49ers and the New Orleans Saints met in room 4096 at the San Francisco Airport Marriott. For five hours the seven men (referee, umpire, linesman, side judge, field judge, line judge and back judge) reviewed game films and went over the referees report from Seeman.

Topics they discussed included how to recognize chop blocks; how to inflate and rub down the 36 new balls (12 for each half and another dozen in reserve) allotted for each game; how to distinguish running into the kicker from roughing the kicker; and what to watch for on sideline passes. "Feet, then ball," Seeman said on a video showing sideline grabs. "Eyes on the feet until they land, then the ball. Feet. Ball."

Each week Seeman and his 10-person staff grade officials by reviewing tapes of all games and then ranking the refs, by position, in relation to each other. The top-rated officials at each position are eligible for postseason assignments. "Peer pressure is our Number 1 motivating factor," says Al Jury, 55, a back judge and veteran of four Super Bowls who recently retired from the California Highway Patrol after 28 years as a patrolman. "We all want to get to the Super Bowl, and to get there you can't be a wimp. You've got to stand up and make the call. I don't think fans appreciate how hard that is."

"It's easy for the world to have an opinion on a call," says Seeman. "They get instant replay. But officials have to make split-second judgments on things that a thousand replays won't always give convincing proof of. Our statistics show officials are correct 95% of the time, and that's pretty damn good."

Avoiding injury is another challenge for officials. Nobody knows this better than umpire Art Demmas. Demmas, 62, is the southern coordinator for the College Football Hall of Fame and is the most senior official in the NFL, now in his 29th year. Umpire is the most dangerous of the seven officiating positions, because umps line up five yards behind

THE GRIDIRON GAME

the defensive line. In 1992, in a game between the Green Bay Packers and the Cincinnati Bengals, Demmas put his hands on his knees and got ready for a play. What happened next is a bad and blurry memory for the ump. There was a running play up the middle, right at him. He was trapped in a pack of linebackers. The ball carrier plowed into the linebackers. Somebody's helmet hit Demmas in the chest. The result: a cracked sternum and severely bruised lungs.

After surgery to repair the damage, Demmas developed pneumonia. His lungs filled with fluid, and they have continued to do so every few days ever since. Because of this condition, called bronchiectasis, Demmas is on antibiotics all the time, and his wife pounds his back to help drain his lungs. "That stuff comes with the job," says Demmas. "I never thought seriously about quitting."

There are some lighter moments on the field as well. Former Bears running back Walter Payton is, by all accounts, the officials' alltime favorite player. Sweetness, as Payton was nicknamed, loved teasing officials, and one of his favorite games was untying their shoelaces. Early in one game Payton surreptitiously undid Frank Sinkovitz's laces so many times that by halftime the official was fuming. Early in the second half, Payton landed on the bottom of a pileup. As Sinkovitz knelt down to break it up, he felt a hand on his foot. He looked down and saw an arm sticking out of the heap, the fingers on his laces.

"Gotcha!" yelled Sinkovitz.

Payton howled with laughter. He said, "What took you so long, Frankie?"

Not every player is an angel, however. Some teams, including the Arizona Cardinals, the Miami Dolphins, the Buffalo Bills and the Oakland Raiders, are notorious for playing so aggressively that officials must always be on guard.

Rick Lipsey

"Everything's on edge with Oakland," says one official. "They are very tough to work."

The toughest thing for an official is to mistakenly impose a penalty. The cardinal rule of NFL officiating is that a no-call is infinitely better than a bad call. Cashion found this out at the end of the first half of Super Bowl XX in 1986. Chicago had driven deep into New England Patriots territory. With 21 seconds remaining in the half, Bears quarterback Jim McMahon scrambled down to the three-yard line. Immediately the Bears lined up, and with three seconds left in the half, their center snapped the ball before Cashion could put it back in play.

Cashion correctly called the Bears for delay of game. But he forgot to run 10 seconds off the clock as a penalty for deliberate clock-stopping in the final two minutes of a half. That would have left no time on the clock. Instead Kevin Butler booted a 24-yard field goal. Fortunately Cashion's error didn't affect the game's outcome; the field goal put the Bears up 23-3 in what would be a 46-10 blowout. Still, Cashion was furious with himself.

"We work so damn hard to make every call," Cashion says. "That's why I can't help but chuckle inside every time I overhear somebody say, 'Why doesn't the NFL use full-time officials?'"

1996

GEORGE PLIMPTON is the author of such books as *Out of My League*, *Paper Lion*, and *The Bogey Man*, and is the editor of *The Paris Review*.

Copyright © 1973 by George Plimpton. Reprinted by permission of Random House.

BILL COSBY is the noted comedian and author of *Childhood*, *Fatherhood*, and *Time Flies*.

Copyright © 1970 by Bill Cosby. Reprinted by permission of William Morris Agency, Inc., on behalf of the author.

WILLIAM GOLDMAN is the sharp-eyed, quick-tongued author of *The Princess Bride*, *Marathon Man*, and *Butch Cassidy and the Sundance Kid*.

From *Wait Till Next Year* by William Goldman and Mike Lupica. Copyright © 1988 by Wiliam Goldman and Mike Lupica. Used by permission of Bantam Books, a division of Bantam Doubleday Dell Publishing Group, Inc.

FREDERICK EXLEY was the winner of the William Faulkner Award for the best first novel of the year, *A Fan's Notes*. His other books include *Last Notes from Home* and *Pages from a Cold Island*.

Excerpted from *A Fan's Notes*. Copyright © 1968 by Frederick Exley.

JIMMY BRESLIN is the author of *World Without End, Amen*, *Table Money*, and most recently, *I Want to Thank My Brain for Remembering Me*. He won the Pulitzer Prize in 1986.

Reprinted by permission of the author.

ALLISON DANZIG was for many years America's premier tennis and football writer for the *New York Times*.

Reprinted by permission of the *New York Times*.

RED SMITH was considered not just a great sportswriter but a great writer who happened to write about sports.

Reprinted by permission.

DAN JENKINS is the author of *Semi-Tough*, *Baja Oklahoma*, and *Fast Copy*, to name but a few.

Reprinted with the permission of Simon and Schuster.

JIMMY CANNON was widely regarded as one of the most distinctive sportswriters of his time and gained a genuine cult of readers in the 1940s, 1950s and 1960s through his syndicated columns in the *New York Post* and *New York Journal-American*.

Reprinted by permission of Henry Holt and Company, Inc.

ROY BLOUNT, JR. is the author of such works as *Camels Are Easy, Comedy is Hard*, *Not Exactly What I Had In Mind*, and *Now Where Are We?*

Reprinted by permission of International Creative Management, Inc.

THOMAS BOSWELL is the syndicated columnist for the *Washington Post* and author of *Strokes of Genius*, *The Heart of the Order*, and *Cracking the Show*.

From *Gameday* by Tom Boswell. Copyright © 1990 by Washington Post Writers Group. Used by permission of Doubleday a division of Bantam Doubleday Dell Publishing Group, Inc.

JIM MURRAY has been honored by the National Sportscasters and Sportswriters Association as Sportswriter of the Year a record 14 times.

Reprinted by permission of the *Los Angeles Times*.

STEVE HUBBARD is a senior writer for *Inside Sports* magazine.

Reprinted by permission of Michael Friedman Publishing Group, Inc.

PAT CONROY is the author of such distinguished works as *The Great Santini*, *The Prince of Tides*, and *Beach Music*.

Reprinted by permission of the author.

THE GRIDIRON GAME

ED LINN is the author of *Hitter*, *Steinbrenner's Yankees*, and *Masque of Honor*, a novel.

Reprinted by permission.

IRA BERKOW still writes for the *New York Times* and is the author of *Hank Greenberg* and *Beyond the Dream*.

Reprinted by permission of the *New York Times*.

JIM BROWN is still the greatest running back of all-time and author of *Out of Bounds*, his autobiography.

Reprinted by permission.

CHRIS COBBS is a sportswriter for the *Los Angeles Times*.

Reprinted by permission of the *Los Angeles Times*.

CHRIS DUFRESNE is a sportswriter for the *Los Angeles Times*.

Reprinted by permission of the *Los Angeles Times*.

TOM JUNOD is a writer-at-large for *GQ*.

Copyright © 1994 Tom Junod. Montana Fading Out first appeared in *GQ*. Reprinted by permission.

BILL PLASCHKE writes a weekly column for the *Los Angeles Times*.

Reprinted by permission of the *Los Angeles Times*.

PAT JORDAN is the author of *False Spring*, *The Cheat*, and *Broken Patterns*, among others.

Reprinted by permission of the author.

TIM GREEN, former defensive end for the Atlanta Falcons, is a featured color analyst for Fox Sports and author of three novels, *Titans*, *Ruffians*, and *Outlaws*.

Reprinted by permission of Warner Books, Inc.

RICK LIPSEY is Senior Writer for *Sports Illustrated*.

Reprinted courtesy of *Sports Illustrated*, 10/14/96. Copyright © 1996, Time Inc. "How Zebras Get Their Stripes" by Rick Lipsey. All rights reserved.

About the Author

Dick Wimmer is the author of the highly acclaimed novel, *Irish Wine* and such great non-fiction works as *The Schoolyard Game* and *The Sandlot Game* and the TV movie, *The Million Dollar Infield*, starring Rob Reiner. His second novel, *Boyne's Lassie*, will appear next spring.